FEARLESS:

WOMEN'S JOURNEYS TO SELF-EMPOWERMENT

|||||||||||||||||||||||||||||||||||||||||||||||||||||||||||||||||||||||||||||||||||||||||||||

EDITED BY CAT PLESKA

Fred,
Thanks for
being such
a great friend!
Love,
Wendy

ISBN: 978-1-09371559-0

The following pieces were previously published:

"My Friend Loraine Asks Will I Go With Her to a Drag Show" first printed in *Rascal*

"Badasses" first printed in *Sheila-Na-Gig*

"I Was a Coal Miner's Wife" first appeared on the blog appfellows.org/ appfellows-blog/2019/1/30/i-was-once-a-coal-miners-wife

Edited by Cat Pleska

Cover and book design by Elizabeth Ford

Line Editor: Michele Schiavone

Etchings by Esther Machio

Photo credits as indicated

Mountain State Press

Published by Mountain State Press, Inc.

Mountainstatepress.org

Scott Depot, WV 25560

Acknowledgments

I invited women to submit pieces to this anthology and as I read them, I'd end up feeling goose bumps rise on my arms in reaction. What became clear is that each woman described when and where they burned into what they have become, hard-won successes, endurance, the moments of self-empowerment, changes that meant: now, I can go on and become what I need to be.

So, I want to acknowledge all the women in this book who so generously allowed us to view their growth, their fights and battles, and the recognition of their own power.

Many thanks to my line editor, Michele Schiavone, and graphic artist Liz Ford.

I'd also like to acknowledge advisors to me, the women (and a man or two) who always listened and commented/responded: Phyllis Wilson Moore, Daniel Pleska, Eliot Parker, Marc Harshman, Laura Bentley, Diana Hume George, and my massage therapist, Taylor Brammer. Not only does she keep me in shape to endure much of what comes at me, she also is a good listener. Her feedback to my ramblings I engage in when I'm upon her table confirm I'm making a bit of sense after all.

Dedication

This anthology is dedicated to Mountain State Press, Inc., a 501 (c) 3 enduring nonprofit that has published West Virginians and Appalachians for forty-one years.

This anthology is dedicated to all the women included in this book, contributors and commenters, those who reviewed and provided blurbs.

This anthology is dedicated to my mom, my aunts, my grandmothers, my women cousins, my women friends and to my beautiful, strong daughter Katie.

Contents

Introduction

When I was 11 or 12, a cousin gave me a couple books to read from his sci-fi collection. I read the cult classic *Alas, Babylon*! It's about the destruction of the earth through nuclear annihilation (written during the height of the Cold War years) and escaping to a new world, which in this book is in Florida. The story sparked my imagination and soon I was daydreaming about the same scenario. Except, in my mental movie I was the leader, gathering people who were panicked and fleeing to my rocket ship to find a new planet. I piloted it, I became captain, and I got us safely to a new home. There, I remained in the leadership role helping everyone to settle.

Somehow or other I missed the message that typically women were rarely in those kinds of roles back in the day. Not in literature or in real life. At least, none of the literature I was exposed to. The usual white males were the saviors, and if women were present, they became the love interest and nothing more. I may not have characterized it as such when I was young, but I did have real-world strong women in my life growing up. They didn't pilot Earth-escaping ships, but they showed me their strength daily.

As I grew older, I became more aware, as the inheritor of feminism and Civil Rights rhetoric, that women rarely appeared in leadership roles, and even more rare was the woman of color, and all paid high prices if they were in these roles. They wouldn't marry or have families and endured the derisive male commentary (as all women have done) and often worse.

Despite my early visions of myself as world savior, self-empowerment was long in coming; after all, the tide against it has been incredibly strong and mostly unquestioned. Finding my inner strength came in bits and pieces, always moving forward to a new way of being. I am witnessing, as I'm sure you are, the re-dedication of women all over the world to be equal, to find equity and embrace it and to live it every day.

The stories in this collection are not about hating men or the system that persists where women are still expected to be homemakers, or mothers, or even cis-gender. These stories are about women knowing they have a longer road to walk and how they got to where they needed to be. They made changes. Or they were changed. Forever.

As editor, I wanted to include women in all ways I could. Besides 30 women contributors in poem, story, and essay, I invited 30 more women to each read one piece I assigned and to provide a 2–3 sentence commentary, like a mini review. I also sought all women to provide blurbs, but of course, I welcome reviews of any gender.

As you read each of these pieces, keep this thought close to your heart: you can do this too if you need and want to. Maybe you already have, for which I recognize you and say: Brava!

As a special note, take a closer look at the symbols on the cover of this book. The graphic artist, Elizabeth Ford, a strong, self-empowered woman, created graphics that represent all manner of the feminine. There are **circles** that represent connections and cycles of life; the **compass** to symbolize guidance and finding your way; **triple moon** meaning a Pagan/Wiccan symbol for maiden, mother, and the crone, as well as cycles of the moon, femininity and transformation; the **eye**, for wisdom and knowledge; **Venus**, a common symbol for female; and finally **Aphrodite's flower**, the flower of life representing the power of transformation and love. The deep purple was the color chosen for 2019's International Year of the Woman.

Perfect.

— CAT PLESKA, Editor

Little girls with dreams become women with vision.
— Author Unknown

You Do Not Have to be Good

after *Wild Geese* by Mary Oliver

SHERRELL WIGAL

||||||||||||||||||||||||||||||||||||||||||||||||||||||||||||

You do not have to mother
every tear-streaked child
or broken woman searching for backbone, strong legs;
To heal each broken necked pigeon
your daughter drags home;
To be the Christmas Eve way-station
for the stranded couple the boss
is afraid to take to his own home;

No need to envy
the blessing of wild geese
over Rochester, Minnesota.

Though these have brought joy
in those moments of attention,
someday you will weigh their cost,
wonder - was there more?

You have only:
To bathe this body given,
the skin of your infants;
To thank the beginning and end of each day;
Remove stiff shoes in spring, walk gently,
let bare feet offer devotions
to expectant soil.

Perhaps years from now,
you might lift auburn eyes,
as Canada geese
chevron the blue dome
over West Virginia.

Through carefully chosen words, the poet encourages readers to move beyond
expectations and "let bare feet offer devotions to … soil"—advice only a West
Virginia farm girl would give. Sherrell's poems always challenge and inspire me.

— WILMA STANLEY ACREE, Poet and Editor

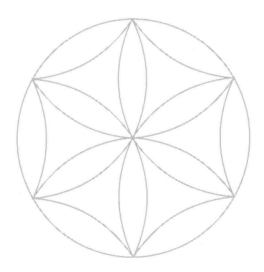

Into the Fire

JANICE GARY

I used to play with fire. It was a strange thing for a teenage girl to do, but seventeen is a strange time in a girl's life. And I was a strange girl.

I had been a strange kid, too—doing my best to fit in, but I never did. My clothes were the wrong clothes, my religion the wrong religion, my family odd in the insular, tightly-wound way of abusive households. To escape reality, I retreated to the world of fairy tales where everything that went wrong went right eventually. Cinderella was my favorite, not just because she got her Prince but because her situation was sad and hopeless and ended up better than she ever dreamed it could be. It was an instructive story for me. I wanted my life to change. And I needed to believe it could.

In the seventh grade, something happened that set in motion my own Cinderella moment. I played the lead in the school production of *The Crucible* and crushed it. I was so convincing that kids called me the name of the character in the play for weeks. Usually, I would be ashamed of that—and I was some—but as a girl who felt she was invisible, I was also rather pleased to be seen. There was something else that happened on that stage. I escaped into the character, became her. It was incredible not to be me for a while. A plan began forming in my head. I already knew I could sing and now that I could act, I would use my talent to transform myself from nobody to somebody. An actress. A singer. A star.

The dream kept me going through difficult times. *Someday*, I kept telling myself, *someday* I would be bigger, brighter, better than anyone. Now that I was seventeen it was time to put the plan into action. My fairy tale had morphed into an intricate fiction involving rock and roll music, long-haired boys and adoring crowds, but the end game was the same. I still wanted to be a star. A *big* star.

And for that, I needed magic.

I waited until everyone in the house was asleep and dragged my nightstand out into the center of my bedroom. As instructed in Sybil Leek's *Diary of a Witch*, I placed a candle on the nightstand-turned-altar, lit it and watched the sputtering wick spring into full flame. Into the fire I went, carrying my secret selves—the girl of silence, the child of pain, the almost-woman I was. My eyes fixed on the flickering blue heart of the flame until I had the guts to bring my index finger close to the candle, then closer, then into the flame.

I watched my finger disappear into the flame with a kind of detached fascination. The instructions made clear that maintaining the same slow, steady pace was vitally important—no hesitation, no stopping midway. I willed myself to stay the course, guiding my finger slowly toward the wick, past it and through the flame until it exited out the other side.

For a moment, I couldn't move. It should have been impossible to go through fire and not feel a thing, but that was exactly what happened. I tried again. Like before, my finger sailed through without any sensation of heat or discomfort. I examined it from all angles; there were no burn marks, only a faint circle of black char that disappeared when swiped across my tee shirt. The skin was perfect, as if it never touched the fire at all.

But of course, it had.

Two years earlier, my father killed himself in our driveway by tying a garden hose to the tail pipe of his car and stuffing it through the driver's window. It was an act of spontaneous combustion. After his death, everything changed, just like that.

We moved to a new state, a new town, a new house and told everyone he had a heart attack. With the insurance money, my mother bought me the teen dream bedroom I had wanted all my life with a four poster bed and matching French provincial furniture. I spent hours locked in my pink shag-carpeted cocoon working on my metamorphosis—playing guitar, writing songs and expanding my mind, both experimentally (pot, LSD) and by reading voraciously about the metaphysical world— everything from Edgar Cayce and his psychic predictions to the Kabbala (which my Rabbi refused to talk about) to the I Ching with its roll-of-the-dice wisdom. I even ordered pamphlets from the Rosicrucians, a quasi-Christian order who sent me literature featuring old guys with long beards in monk-like robes—which both intrigued and repelled me.

Then I stumbled on Sybil Leek, a British woman who built a cottage industry of witch guidebooks in the 1970s. She called herself a witch, but her practice was Wicca, also known as white witchcraft. It was a perfect storm of magic, mysticism and female power. Although I was a budding "women's libber," it was Leek's books that opened my eyes to the violent suppression of women as part of an effort to eradicate the old, feminine religions. It turned out witches were not the evil, ugly hags my fairy tales had warned of, but women of healing and power who communed with the moon and the stars and the natural world. It sounded good to me. I decided to give it a try.

The Witches' Guidebook was a complete lifestyle manual which included recipes for healing teas and tips for natural beauty among the spells and rituals. Although I'm sure I must have sampled other lessons in magic, the only one I recall practicing was the test of fire, which for seventeen-year-old me must have seemed like an epic battle of faith over fear. Mastering the flame proved I could do anything. However hot it would get, I could take the heat.

Or so I thought.

How much fire is needed to forge a witch? Certainly more than one scented candle's worth. Passing through the flame once or twice was a party trick compared to the tests I would face as a woman. My initiation was just beginning.

As I entered the world, I had to face many fires—the bonfire of rape, the slow burn of Post-Traumatic Stress, the kindling created by depression and obsessive thoughts, the fear, the violence, the red-hot embers of a combustible childhood. I've walked over white-hot coals with my naked soul in order to walk the streets alone. Be believed. Find my voice and use it. Writing about it almost seems like an impossible task. How do you sweep the ash of so many smoldering remnants into one place to make a neat little pile on the page?

"The first rule of magic," author Julia Cameron writes, "is containment."

The page is a container. It offers a safe house for my words. I'm never sure I can do what it asks of me, especially here, buried beneath this charred wreck of a story. But I'll try.

Not long after my finger passed through the flame, I headed out to California to blaze a path to stardom. I put together a promising band of other hopefuls and played solo gigs in tiny coffeehouses on stages the size of two chairs and a microphone stand. With no car and no money I walked everywhere or hitched rides, which was stupid but necessary. One night, I walked to a friend's house in fog so thick that houses disappeared in the shroud, seen only by their dimly glowing porch lights and windows. As I stopped and moved closer to one of those porch lights to make out the house number, a man came out of the shadows, grabbed me by the throat and threatened to kill me. As my body went limp, he dragged me into a garage where he slammed me against a car and stole the singer in me. After the rape, my insides were so inflamed I had to soak in water for half an hour a day for two weeks. On the street, unexpected sounds or quick movements ignited alarm bells throughout my body that literally left me shaking with fear.

Being a star was no longer such a priority. I just wanted to make sure I could make it to my front door without being taken down.

Rape is a kerosene-soaked rag thrown into a life. An explosion that shocks and stuns and then sets off smaller fires that burn for a long time. Although I learned how to cover my injuries and pretend there were no scars, the Post Traumatic Stress I endured raged unchecked and undiagnosed for thirty years.

But it was not the first fire. That happened much earlier. You learn as a girl about female powerlessness in ways big and small. In my home, my father was the king and my mother a doormat he wiped his boots on. Nightly, I learned every belittling, hurtful word there was for a woman. I witnessed beatings, punches and threats and explosive temper tantrums where furniture, glasses and dining tables were thrown across the room or smashed against walls. I saw my mother as weak, my father as needy and so I filled his neediness with flattery, admiration and good little girlness. I went on dates with him where he taught me how to be a "lady," to let a man open the doors for me, order my dinner, pull out my chair to sit down, to get up, to get out. I was not to be crude—no whistling or farting or picking my nose—all of which I liked to do.

And I was to sleep with him while my mother slept on the couch. My father never physically molested me, except for the one time he accidentally did—or must have. I was asleep when he kicked me out of bed and said we couldn't do *this* anymore. I did not know what *this* was, but I do know as I got up and walked out of that bedroom, I felt the thick heat of shame cover me. That shame followed me everywhere I went. To make sure I would not forget what kind of person I was, I wrote down the worst names my father called my mother and hid them in my dresser drawer. Whenever I saw them or thought of them, the shame flamed up again. And again. I could not escape the horrible not-to-be-done thing I had done. At twelve, my body was preparing to change from girl to woman. And to be a woman, I learned, was a shameful thing.

I look back at this as the time the fires in my head started. The incident in my father's bed turned on the obsessive-compulsive switch in my brain, which still overheats if not kept in check by medication. Depression is another slow burn, one I tried to ignore for a long time, until I couldn't anymore. Even so, I tried to control it on my own—taking medication, then not, being okay, then being very not okay. My mother, a lifelong depressive herself, said *it's all in your head*. Ironically, it was.

Each time depression sparked a major breakdown, it left kindling behind—that's an actual technical term for the neurons burned to a crisp from a major depressive episode. Kindling means that if a fire erupts again, it will be bigger than the last one. It means I walk around with dry tinder in my brain, waiting to go up in flames.

Women are twice more likely to suffer from depression and anxiety disorders as men[1]; they have higher rates of multiple psychiatric disorders, higher rates of bipolar disorder[2], higher rates of developing depression and anxiety as a result of childhood abuse or sexual trauma[3]. Hippocrates was certain all ailments suffered by women resulted from their "wandering wombs." As bizarre as this sounds, modern medicine and psychiatry—for all its advances—often continues to treat a woman's body and mind as a mysterious vessel of "imagined" injuries. For millennia, the effects of gender violence, inequity and societal repression have been explained away as "hysteria."

Imagine that.

When my body began feeling like it was on fire, I didn't know what was happening, but I did know that I pushed myself and pushed myself and ignored my pain while attending to the needs of others— my husband, my siblings, my mother, my job, my boss, my own insistent need to be someone, do something. I had given up on the famous star dream but not on making something of myself and doing so while enduring an unending struggle with undiagnosed PTSD, the unconscious trauma of a violent childhood, the unrelenting demands of being female in a male world and the unspoken rage that simmers just under a woman's skin.

It wasn't until I had spent years of struggling with fatigue, insomnia and the throbbing pain of overheated nerve endings that I heard about Fibromyalgia. All the symptoms matched mine, but the illness was one with no real cure or even a definitive diagnosis. Fibromyalgia was mainly a "woman's disease" and I have no doubt that's why for years there was debate about whether it even existed. Sometimes *I* even wondered if it was. When the medical community finally acknowledged that it was caused by inflammation, it wasn't news to me: my body was on fire. Mine and that of many other women who had been told their pain was imaginary.

We are not supposed to notice when we hurt.

We are not supposed to complain.

We are not supposed to resist.

When I was raped, the advice from law enforcement was to *relax and enjoy it*. No wonder so many of us are on fire.

While I'm writing about burning women, my body is burning. Not just from Fibromyalgia, which comes and goes and happens to be present today, but from the rage—the absolute outrage at how pervasive and hidden and destructive the damage has been—and still is—from the out of control fires of a patriarchy gone mad. Here's a short list: brides burned, women raped, girls put into sexual slavery, stalked, shamed, shut up, grabbed and beaten, killed, set on fire, disfigured by acid attacks. Many of these crimes are committed by husbands or ex-husbands or ex-lovers or some man they barely know who cannot take "no" for an answer. The men who do this often walk away. Sometimes they become Supreme Court justices. Or even President.

It's hard to contain such rage once you've discovered how to scream.

On the stage in the sixth grade as Anne Putnam in *The Crucible* I screamed as loud as my lungs would let me, accusing innocent girls and women of being witches. I remember how good it felt to let those screams go. But it took many decades and my own trials with fire before I could find a strong voice of my own.

I still like to dance in the moonlight. To watch the seasons change and witness the changes in myself as they come and go. I have been tried by fire and tested by the dark. I don't know if that makes me a witch, but it does make me a woman who knows how to burn and not be destroyed.

If that's not magic, I don't know what is.

<hr />

In her essay, Janice Gary brews a remarkable potion to counter the powerlessness and self-loathing she learned at the hands of an abusive father. Tossed into the cauldron are the ingredients of her life: a fascination with fire and *The Crucible*, white witchcraft and star dreams, her father's suicide and a brutal rape at the hands of a stranger. The stew also holds the fallout of her trauma: PTSD and a brain littered with combustible kindling. But Gary's potion is strong, and she is resilient and protected by her own good magic.

— MARIE MANILLA, Author of *Patron Saint of Ugly*

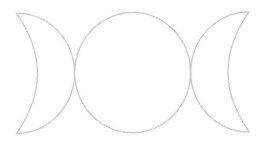

The Girl in the Mirror

CARTER TAYLOR SEATON

A large maple-framed mirror hung over the couch in my childhood home. Each time I passed through the living room I glanced at the mirror, hoping to see that the flat-chested girl had magically blossomed into a ravishing beauty. And each time, my mother would tell me not to be so conceited. I remember her asking me once—I'd apparently voiced my fears that I'd never be pretty like other girls—if I'd rather be smart or beautiful. I said I wanted both. After that I clearly understood that she didn't think both were possible and that smart was to be my only role.

When I disappointed my parents by becoming pregnant as a high school junior, her reaction was one more affirmation that I hadn't measured up to Mother's notion of what girls were supposed to do or be in the 1950s. She told me I'd broken Daddy's heart, but I think it was hers that was broken. Her dream for me had always been a good marriage and children because that's what she knew, but Daddy had always told me I could be anything I wanted, and I still believed him. So, when I got pregnant, she made me continue in the church pageant role of the Virgin Mary, so she wouldn't lose face by having to explain why I wanted to drop out.

Being more practical, Daddy arranged a quick wedding—minus the shotgun. He then found a way for me to enroll in a new high school since I'd been asked to leave Huntington High School because, pregnant, I would be a "distraction." I wanted badly to continue my education and he wasn't going to let a little thing like pregnancy stop me. That summer, in the full bloom of impending motherhood, I attended classes at the Marshall Lab School, finishing my eleventh-grade requirements two days before the birth of my first son. That fall, he became my first-period home economics class child-care project until my mother picked him up so I could finish the rest of the day's classes. I graduated on-time and went on to Marshall College the following January, after the birth of my second son, and the divorce that preceded it by one day.

To my knowledge no one has discovered a gene for self-determination. I don't think they will, either. I believe that a person's self-determination springs instead from facing and overcoming challenges, from emulating role models, or from rebelling against becoming someone they identify as their anti-hero.

When I was in my early-twenties, a female friend attending a party my husband and I hosted was bragging about her weekly accomplishments. Her husband was a doctor and she'd been a nurse who supported the family while he was in medical school. Now with three boys and a girl, her life consisted of attending Little League games and taking care of the children. As she boasted of how clean she got her boys' jock straps, I thought, *Dear Lord, please let me have something else in my life to talk about besides that.* I had four children too, but to me, she had lost her identity as a woman, and was simply being a mother and wife, not that there's anything wrong with it. However, the fact that she took a thermos of Scotch with her to those ballgames was a good clue that she wasn't fulfilled in her chosen or assigned role. She became the anti-hero who spurred my determination to do more with my life.

Then, there are my sheros. Take my Aunt Nancy. At twenty-seven, when her two younger brothers enlisted in the Army early in World War II, she argued that women should serve as well. Against her father's wishes, she enlisted in the Women's Army Auxiliary Corps and served in the then-secret field of radar. Or my Aunt Elinore who, after graduating from college with an English Literature degree but no business skills, opened a riding academy in order to earn enough money to take her and her sister to Europe. Later in life these gutsy women led fights against racism, discrimination, unfair housing practices, mountaintop removal mining, and other atrocities that oppressed their fellow humans. Elinore even shaved her head in protest, saying "hair grows back; mountaintops don't."

After I married again at nineteen, I continued attending college, determined to get my degree. But when my youngest son was in the third grade, I put school on hold and broke the proverbial young-woman mold again by going to work. Daddy asked me who was going to fix my four kids their snacks after school if I wasn't there. I told him that I guessed they'd have to learn for themselves where the bread, peanut butter, and jelly were. Previously, I'd volunteered for various projects, but had never been employed a day in my life. Nevertheless, I was tapped to become the executive director of a nascent non-profit craft-cooperative. I think it was 'fake-it-until-you-make-it' thinking that allowed me to take on that challenge. Despite my lack of business acumen, I persevered and learned how to run a business. This on-the-job training also allowed me to earn the requirements for my Regents' BA Degree.

Finally, after two more children and a fifteen-year career as the director of that non-profit organization, I graduated from Marshall University in 1982. I had managed to beat my children by four years. And I was single, again, but I'd learned that I could make my own way. The divorce had been my choice, but one I didn't make lightly.

As the marriage was breaking down, I began running as a way to clear my head. I never expected it to become an integral part of my life, but after I moved to Columbus, Georgia, I began entering short races. At a party after one race, someone I was introduced to said, "Oh, you're a runner, aren't you?" I said yes, but in my heart, I knew I was just a dabbler in the sport. I thought to myself, *no, I'm not, but I'm going to be someday.*

Three years later, I moved to Atlanta, the mecca for southern runners. Every part of the city had a running club. The granddaddy of them all was the Atlanta Track Club. I joined it as well as one in the Marietta area where I'd bought a townhouse. Soon I was running five days a week, entering races right and left, including the infamous Peachtree Road Race that ends in Piedmont Park after a grueling uphill climb near Piedmont Hospital. One day I was asked if I'd ever run a marathon—26.2 miles—and I laughed. "Are you kidding? I'm doing well to cover six miles. No way." Next thing I knew, I was training for the Atlanta Marathon on Thanksgiving Day 1990. I finished, and wasn't last, but I was hooked. I signed on with a running coach, attended a weeklong running camp in Asheville, and ran two more marathons after I was fifty: New York City, and Marine Corps. There's a saying in running: plan your race, and race your plan. It's good wisdom. As a back-of-the-pack runner, I was only competing against myself. Challenging myself to do better each time. Mentally seeing myself cross the finish line. I was never fast, but perseverance kept me going. No way would I have dropped out regardless of how hard it was.

Some challenges present themselves, like coping with an alcoholic husband or ending life support for your oldest son, and you grapple to overcome them. Others you willingly accept. My brother invited me to join his family on a scuba-diving vacation in the Cayman Islands with this remark: "You need to take diving lessons first." I accepted his invitation but told him I'd learn down there. Although I caught my dive jacket on a wreck when I was training, I was never frightened of being one-hundred feet below the surface. The same sort of saying applies to diving: plan your dive, and dive your plan. It will keep you alive a whole lot longer.

One evening at dinner I told my close friend, Allison, a story about my family. She was astonished and told me I should write a book about it.

"I write press releases," I told her. "I've never written anything creative."

An artist who never shied away from a challenge herself, she said "Well, it's time you started."

And so, I did. Fifteen years later my writing career still challenges me. Each project presents a new one. I think of each new project as a race, a dive; I see myself with the finished book in my hands.

When I look back over the past sixty-plus years, I realize that making it through some of those tough situations—mostly of my own making—as a young girl gave me the courage to tackle big challenges as an adult. When a person learns that I was married and divorced by age seventeen; that by age twenty-three I had four children under the age of six, or that I held a full-time job and dealt with teenage hippie-wannabe sons in the 1970s, they ask, "How did you do it?" My answer is always the same. Life is like running a marathon. Accept new challenges. Set new goals. And no matter what obstacle you face in reaching that goal, remember my running mantra: *you can do anything for just one more block; for just one more mile; for just one more minute; for just one more hour; for just one more day. That's my definition of self-determination.*

The stories we tell are the sense we make. In her telling, Carter threads the sources of her courage into inspiration for moving with and through life challenges. "The Girl in the Mirror" not only models the growth that comes from navigating a path with courage, but also reflects the writing life as a means for charting the course.

— BETH DARBY, Writer

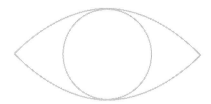

Knowing What it Takes

KAREN SALYER MCELMURRAY

Recently, I was part of a panel discussion on strong women called "Kiss My Grits: On the Badass in Appalachian Literature." It was easy to think of any number of strong women who are badass in the books I love most from the mountains. Gertie Nevel in Harriet Arnow's *The Dollmaker* came to mind first, followed closely by other strong women characters like Carrie Marie Mullins in Mary Ann Taylor Hall's *Come and Go Molly Snow,* Serena Pemberton in Ron Rash's *Serena,* or most recently, Dawn Jewell in Robert Gipe's *Trampoline.* But as days passed and I thought more and more about what I'd say about strong women characters based on the place I'm from, it was the word "badass" that tripped me up again and again, and I did the thing I encourage my writing students not to do. I went to look up that word in the dictionary.

I told myself I was being really hip by choosing a funny, badass even, dictionary that would give me a fun spin on our topic— Urbandictionary.com. This is what I found. *Badass.* The epitome of the American Woman. She radiates confidence in everything she does, whether it's ordering a drink, buying a set of wheels, or dealing with men. She's slow to anger, brutally efficient when fighting back. *The badass.* She carves her own path. She wears, drives, drinks, watches, and listens to what she chooses, when she chooses, where she chooses, uninfluenced by fads or advertising campaigns. *Badass.* A style that is understated but instantly recognizable. Like a chopped Harley or a good pair of sunglasses. *Badass.* Simple, direct, and functional.

This definition made me flinch, not because I don't like the idea of confidence and radiating it on my own chosen path in life while sporting leather pants and a nice do rag, but some of the other language? *Brutally efficient. Simple. Direct. Functional* even. Sounds too much like Biker Barbie for me. So I went back to the drawing board, Wikipedia this time, and found a shorter definition. Badass. Tough, uncompromising, intimidating. I liked that one a little better. There was something called The Free Dictionary, which described a tough or aggressive person. The meanest *badass* in town. A *badass* rock band. A real *badass* watch. And Merriam Webster, the one I always had my students avoid? *Badass.* Ready to cause or get into trouble. Mean. Pretending to be a *badass* gunslinger. Of formidable strength or skill.

Strength was at least something I could get my teeth around, the self I had always wanted most, and above all the definition I could lay hands on when it came to some of the women I grew up around. My great-aunt Della, my mother's aunt, fixed brakes, changed oil, fried eggs, paid the bills. It was the 1960s. When I was little we'd drive home to Eastern Kentucky and sit in the booths at Della's place, a service station and diner called the Black Cat. A photograph I have of the diner is of a shelf full of cartons of Winstons and Salems with my great-grandmother seated at a booth. That great grandmother, Beck, lived in a room off that diner until she passed. Della. Her sun-browned face and her sad, fierce eyes. Della, they said, was odd-turned. *Contrary.* I've written stories about her, her big hands, black-streaked and strong from the hard work they did. I imagine her reaching down into some vat of soaking spark plugs, some geography of wires and hoses. Later, when I learned to gap plugs and change my Dodge Dart's oil, I thanked my memories of Della. She was strong enough to run a business, skilled enough to manage a garage and a restaurant. Strong enough to lock the doors when my uncle Russell came home drunk. He fell asleep one winter night with his truck's engine running and they found him dead of carbon monoxide fumes that early morning.

I remember other strong, skilled women in my family. There was Rita Wallen, a cousin and niece of Della's, from up toward Pikeville. I didn't spend much time with Rita when I was growing up, but she was someone I heard a lot of stories about. Rita, they said, had book smarts.

She did good in high school, even better in college, went on to some school up north and became, so the family said, a Big Lawyer, though she didn't come back home much over the years afterwards. Another woman of strength and, they said, dubious skills, was Betty, my Uncle Roy's first wife. Roy and Betty lived in a brick house he built down in the bottom land below my grandparents' house, and they raised a garden, had a little girl, but Betty hankered after something she didn't have. They said it was more of this, more of that, a new couch, a sip of whiskey on the sly, but the Betty I remember styled her hair in a frosted shag. She bought shiny white go-go boots and took off for Ohio in the middle of the night, became a dancer in a juke joint and never came back again.

I could go on all day remembering other women I grew up around who fit the definition of badass as someone strong and also ready to cause trouble or get into it or maybe just survive it. I could tell you about a great grandmother who smoked a pipe and survived two husbands, one killed by, so the stories go, a Floyd County gunslinger. I could tell you about a grandmother who hoed an acre big garden, an aunt who worked triple shifts at the Double Kwik to take care of her family, a cousin who drove an hour a day there and back to go to community college to become a social worker. All those stories of perseverance and strength and, okay, badassery. But the more I thought about definitions, the more I kept coming back to something quieter, another word in our panel description. *Unseen.* Invisible, even. The kind of strength you see if you look at the eyes, at the palms of the hands. The kind of strength you see in the ripped and mended places in the spirit. That kind of badass.

There is a phrase that comes to me again and again about certain women I have known, been friends with, kin to, akin to, is something like this. She is, I will think to myself, someone who someone has done something to. That's a terrible thing to know in your gut when you meet or spend time with someone. There's the cousin I'll call Kristine, the one who had her first baby when she was sixteen, and everyone knew Kristine's child belonged to her own daddy, who ended up in prison for statutory rape. You know she had to do something to bring that on her own self, my own grandmother said, and I bit my tongue to hold back from saying something, saying, look at her, just look. Look how she had that baby, and then walked on from there, went back to school, became a hairdresser, had other babies. I wish I could tell you more about her life, but I only know that when I see her, her eyes are steady, her voice one of the calmest I have known. There's my cousin Jenny, dead now, but her story too is one I walk around with. Jenny, weighing in at three hundred pounds, then down to one fifty, back up again so big that time she had to ride a motor cart when she went to Wal-Mart to buy her packs of powdered sugar donuts, the ones she loved so much. Her mother, my aunt, schizophrenic, living in a home for the disabled, the differently abled as they say it now. Her daughter, Michaela, wild as a hare, bipolared out, dead at twenty, a suicide. But Jenny picked up, packed up, moved to Cincinnati. Is that running away? Is that strength? To leave behind a state, a county line, a town, a house, to move somewhere where the streets were clean and clear, unhistoried, there to find love, watch it settle in her own two hands, even if her body gave out, that last time, when the weight came back and her face blossomed, that time with happiness.

A couple years ago, when I was teaching in a low residency program in Western Kentucky, a colleague and I were talking about memoir. I had just quoted, in a talk, a favorite author of mine, Dorothy Allison, who said this: "I believe the secret of writing is that it never exceeds the reach of the writer's courage. The best writing comes from the place where our terror hides. Until I was writing about exactly the things I was most afraid of and unsure about, I wasn't writing worth a damn." My colleague, a novelist, as we chatted that evening over wine, said that she, too, likes memoir, but she called such works "narratives of victimhood." Maybe this is a matter of semantics, but as you know from my experiences with definitions, I took this definition on too. Victimhood. Narratives. Of. Stories of victims. Victim. A person who has been attacked, injured, robbed, or killed by someone else. A person who is cheated or fooled by someone or something. One that is harmed by an unpleasant event. Well, all of that is true. Kristine. Jenny. Michaela. All of them harmed, injured, robbed even. Still, I do not like the words in my mouth. Narratives of victimhood. I prefer, I find, to come back to our original word for this panel. *Badass.*

Sunday mornings I often read the latest issue of *Brain Pickings Weekly.* A few weeks back I read a piece by a woman named Caroline Paul, from her book called *The Gutsy Girl: A Modern Manifesto for Bravery, Perseverance, and Breaking the Tyranny of Perfection.* Caroline Paul takes on the idea that one must be perfect and error-proof in every way in order to live a daring and courageous life. She talks about her many missteps in her own life, and she assures her readers over and over that owning up to mistakes isn't an attrition of one's courage but an essential building. I quote, "After all, the fear of humiliation is perhaps what undergirds all fear, and in our culture of stubborn self-righteousness there are few things we resist more staunchly, to the detriment of our own growth, than looking foolish for being wrong. The courageous, Paul reminds us, trip and fall, often in public, but get right back up and leap again."

The courageous, to me, don't just trip and fall. They have gotten back up and walked on. They are not victims, but keen and strong survivors. They are vulnerable. We see their experiences, an almost map on their skin, a sometimes weary fire in their eyes, a keening undercurrent in a voice in an empty room, a voice in a car down a road heading out, a voice on a page. In the end, that to me is the definition of badass. Courage, hidden, invisible maybe, but sharp as a blade, a fine-honed bone feather, a will not just to survive, but to live. Those are the women I long to read about, write about and, most importantly, the kind of woman I want to become.

What begins as a deceptively simple meditation on a word ("badass") quickly becomes, for Karen Salyer McElmurray, a more complicated and compelling reconsideration of what it means to be a strong Appalachian woman. This is the kind of woman McElmurray longs to become—the kind she already shows herself to be, with this writing. It takes guts, as this portrait shows, to pull back the curtain and be vulnerable.

— RACHAEL PECKHAM, Author of *Muck Fire*

Poverty Brain

KATHERINE MANLEY

I was six years old when my peg-legged father sold our two-room shack near Charleston, West Virginia, for thirty cans of Wilson's evaporated milk. He moved the family fifty miles away to Logan County where we continued to struggle with poverty. I stood beside him as he sat in front of dime stores and sold pencils in several southern West Virginia towns.

When we weren't street begging, our family carried shopping bags door to door asking for food and clothes. As a child, I spent my summers berry picking and scavenging through dumps to help feed our family. Sometimes I gathered scrap iron to sell or lumps of coal for heat. On a Saturday in early October, during my 9th grade year, my mom could not deal with poverty any longer. She ran away, leaving me to care for my crippled father and younger brother and sister. I didn't even have time to mourn her absence. Between homework, housework, and begging, I had very little time for myself.

In fact, it was a few weeks later before Mom's leaving finally sank in. All the extra chores and caring for the family had worn me down. One day, school seemed to drag on, and I couldn't wait to get home.

The old school bus creaked along, getting closer to my stop. Mr. Browning, my ninth-grade civics teacher, whom I always respected, taught something in class that angered me. It was the first time in my fifteen years that I had ever known a teacher to tell a lie.

The bus rolled to an abrupt stop at the railroad crossing in front of the Island Creek Store. Beside the company store was my destination, the Verdunville Post Office. I decided not to walk home right away. I needed to be alone.

Gracie, our bus driver, flagged the kids who lived behind the company store across the road. She watched them as they hurried across the railroad tracks. Today, I did not follow the others across the tracks. Instead, I headed toward the post office below the store along with a couple of other students.

I shifted my literature and civics books in the cradle of my arms and hurried to the little brown building. The flag flapped in front of the post office as I walked by. The other students went inside to get their family's mail, but I walked to the back of the building. I sat on the ground and stared at the rusty, sudsy creek. I found the page in the civics book that had angered me:

> *"We hold these truths to be self-evident, that all men are created equal, that they are endowed by their Creator with certain inalienable Rights; that among these are Life, Liberty and the pursuit of Happiness."*
> — *Thomas Jefferson, The Declaration of Independence, July 4, 1776*

Tears filled my eyes. Happiness? How could all men be created equal when some people had food and some didn't? Why did our family always run out of food the last week of every month? All around me, people ate sandwiches on their porches every day of the year. Why did my Mom run away and not somebody else's? How was I supposed to be happy when hunger was frequent, and I had to work even harder to take Mom's place and try to get through school? Where was the happiness for me?

I folded my arms across my chest. I closed my eyes and mumbled several times, "All men are *not* created equal!" I remained sitting on the ground for a few more minutes trying to figure it out.

Daddy often spoke of how the Cooks next door afforded many luxuries, including vacations, because Mr. Cook was a coal miner. "They make about eight-hundred dollars a month," he said. "And now, take the Thompsons across the street there. That family gets about three-hundred dollars a month from Social Security. They can buy all the food they want."

I teared up when I remembered the last part Daddy had said. "We're on welfare, so we only get ninety dollars a month. That doesn't divide very well among a family of five." Though not even a family of four, now that my mother was gone..

Tears rolled down my cheeks. Tears that I had saved up for weeks. At that moment, it hit me that, in life, everyone was an eight, a three, or a one based on the amount of money they received each month. The Cooks were 8s, because they received $800 a month. Our family was a *one*, but only if you rounded ninety dollars up to one hundred. We were less than ones.

I sat there a little longer and thought about the way things were. Up until that moment, I never paid much attention to what I wanted to be when I grew up. Although things weren't clear to me, I knew one thing for sure: I did not want to be a one.

During these challenging years, a few teachers took time to encourage me, praise my classroom accomplishments, and give me clothing. So early on, I decided that I wanted to be like them. I wanted to make a difference in the lives of others. From that point on, I would not let anything stop me. More than anything, I wanted to be a guiding light for those who struggled with poverty. In 1971, I was graduated from high school with honors, and nearly eleven years later, I achieved my dream of becoming a teacher.

One of my strengths as a teacher is that I reflect every day upon what I am doing in the classroom, and I am not afraid to adjust my practice when I find a better way. One of the most important things I do for my students is to be there for them. No matter what their home environment or instructional level, I take them as far as they can go. I am their ambassador to the adult world, and I take time to talk to them about their interests—movies, books, music, and TV shows. I want no child to experience the loneliness and isolation I did as a child.

Because my students struggle with poverty and come from homes where the parents' main concern is daily survival, I work hard to get to know them. After determining my students' reading levels, preferences, favorites, and pet peeves, I explain how they became who they are. Then I help them model how to modify their behavior.

Because many of them come from noisy, chaotic environments, this behavior shows up in the classroom. They feel they must "shout" to be heard. I speak to them quietly and model proper speaking at all times. I also teach them how to empathize, so they can understand the feelings of others. I believe empathy mediates aggression which, in turn, allows for a calmer classroom environment, which is conducive to learning. I also create and design lessons with the theme of altruism. I include everyone. No one is allowed to disappear in my room.

My philosophy as an educator is that I must reach all students whether they live on steep hillsides or in deep hollows. As an adult, I see the "good" that came from the hurt and pain of poverty. Those struggling years of yesterday now allow me to show greater empathy toward my students. I freely integrate my life experiences and counseling into my instruction to help students overcome obstacles that may prevent them from learning. All students, not only those in poverty, need a positive role model to help enrich their lives so that they may be successful.

All students are messengers. They go to a future that I will never see, and it is my job to help them carry the right message. As a survivor of poverty, I am especially familiar with my students' struggles and encourage them to set high, worthwhile goals that include furthering their education.

An informative reading that helps me in my classrooms is *A Framework for Understanding Poverty,* by Dr. Ruby K. Payne, Ph.D. She explains the various key roles that families in poverty may play, including the male fighter/lover and female caretaker/rescuer. I explain these roles to my students because I want them to see that generational poverty can stop. I allow a few minutes of small group discussion before a whole group shares. They are quick to point out that education is the key. But I also point out that the female teenager needs education to help her see she does not have to settle for what has been the norm in her family and surrounding families. The serious look on their faces is priceless. I can see the wheels spinning as they absorb the unit on poverty.

When I was a child, I never dreamed of going to college. Being raised in poverty denied me many educational opportunities, but I became an eager learner who enjoyed gaining and sharing knowledge. I now have three college degrees and have been an educator for thirty-seven years. For the past several years, I have tried to be a lifeline, a dedicated source of inspiration and hope, commodities in short supply for many Appalachian children, who because of economic and cultural disadvantages, begin their lives in the same state of relative social invisibility I experienced.

Surely one of the most terrible injustices committed against the poor is the assumption that they are people who will never, ever matter, an assumption so pernicious that all but the strongest of the economically disadvantaged come to believe it about themselves. Unless something occurs early to reverse this attitude, a poverty of both environment and spirit will travel with the initially disadvantaged across the years. They will literally become a silent piece of history unless they find a larger dream.

Teachers and other significant others can help students achieve that dream. Into the morass of inadequate parental support, stifling home environment, limited access to health and dental care, and limited educational resources, virtually no opportunities for the kind of travel that provides educational enrichment, too much exposure to West Virginia dialects rather than standard spoken and written English—into this quagmire they can introduce the power of possibility.

I have known hunger, cold, and loneliness, but school was my best friend and my escape from poverty. I am so thankful for the few teachers that looked beyond the dirt on my skin and into my potential. Because of them, I realized my dream and am *paying it forward.*

We drink fatalism in the water here in southern West Virginia, but I have learned to spit it out.

Compassion is not something that can be learned from a text. It is learned through living, and this is a perfect example. I felt a strong connection to growing up very poor. I, too, sold soda bottles to get cash. Not only did I sell them for 2 cents to 5 cents each, we would all return to the same stores later in the day, steal them from the back steps and sell them to other stores. Children are resourceful!

— INGRID BRILES, Award Winning Writer

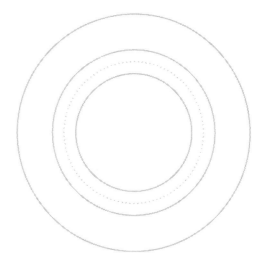

By Grace and Hard Times

KATE DOOLEY

||||||||||||||||||||||||||||||||||||||||||||||||||||

My mother was born at the Spring equinox and often said she didn't know if she was the first breath of spring or the end of a long, hard winter.

She was the smartest person I ever met; she could spell any word you asked her, tell you where to find what in the Bible, knew which wild plant was good to eat, what to do when you stubbed your toe, how to be yourself and not somebody else, and that you shouldn't believe everything the preacher tells you.

On her birth certificate is the name Olive Grace Hall, but she would tell you, "No, that is not my name. I was named Olivia and they put it down wrong."

When she dressed for town, she'd put on her stockings with the seam up the back and take out the bobby pins that she'd slept in all night and brush out her chestnut-colored hair and tuck those curls under a hairnet, take off her floured apron and flowered house dress and put on her town clothes, and rub her hands with a smidgen of Jergens lotion that smelled like burnt almonds. And she'd wear her store-bought teeth. Her real teeth had been knocked out when a truck ran into her on Main Street in September 1953, three months before I was born. Mama would wear high heeled shoes down off that hill, down that dirt road and the cobblestone road and the paved hill street and graveled Little Rocky. A mile and a half to town from up at our place.

I was ten years old, standing in the kitchen doorway, waiting for her to find her pocketbook and count her dollars one more time—and sigh—and mark something off her store list. And then say, "I know what let's do, let's get us a ice cream cone down at the custard stand on our way home."

Coming back, carrying paper pokes full of groceries, we'd wait until we were well up from the valley, after the road turned from pavement to cobbled stones, then off would come her shoes and she'd roll her stockings down, balancing on one foot and then the other, her hand on my shoulder to steady herself as she slipped them off.

Those stones were smooth and as cool as the river they came from long back in Mama's younger days. Her own dad worked on that road, "And Phurah did, too," she'd say. "He's a hard worker when ... " and her voice would drift off and not finish the sentence she'd started to tell about my dad.

She said, "People around here, back when I was your age, they used to raise hogs and cows and they'd just turn them loose to fend for themselves all summer. You had to be ready to run if one of them took a notion to come after you."

She'd look up the road to where the big oaks lay down heavy shadows in the turn of the bend—I knew the ghost stories that came with those trees—but those weren't the stories she was telling now. She was seeing those cows and half-wild hogs coming up on her and her sisters as they walked to Sunday meeting or when they moseyed home from school.

She didn't say so at the time, but those roaming cows caused her miscarriage and the loss of her third child. She'd taken Donald and Junior, my oldest siblings, on a picnic down by the river to get out of the house a bit and enjoy the good weather. I know exactly how that came about without ever being told. The little boys would have been fussy, cooped up inside the house, and Mom would have stopped her work and said, "I know what let's do..." and off they would have gone with their biscuits spread with jam to enjoy the day down by the river. That's all it should have ever been, but as the boys played at the water's edge, an angry bull came charging at them and she grabbed both her sons and made for the hills. The stillborn infant, Daisy, was about the size of a teaspoon, and they buried her under the apple tree behind Grandma and Grandpa Hall's house.

Mom didn't tell that story—some things were too sad to tell—but our lives were full to brimming with remembered hints of other days.

I'd help her hang laundry on the line and she'd tell me about when she worked at the clothespin factory. We'd be mopping floors and she'd tell me how they used to do it by throwing sand on the wooden floor and scrubbing with a broom and sweeping the water out the door or down through the cracks and knotholes. They kept scrubbing until that floor was sanded as smooth as alabaster.

"My first job was at a funeral parlor," she told me once. "I didn't work there too long."

She was cleaning the place after hours, had swept and mopped and was about to do the dusting and didn't have a cloth and figured there must be cleaning cloths there somewhere, so she opened up a big drawer on a cabinet built into the wall. And promptly closed it. She laughed then, telling it, that laugh that was part Cheshire cat, part Muttley the cartoon hound.

"What was in that drawer?" I asked her.

"Oh." (And that laugh again.) You don't want to know."

Mom's stories never had endings; they were just snippets of things as they occurred to her. It might be the way the sun shone through the open doorway that brought something to mind, or how a breeze stirred the leaves on the birch tree in the yard. Or blackberries getting ripe and fat and filling the air with the smell of luxury, all sugar and tang.

"There was this one time," she told me, "when me and Lorena and Ruth were a'visiting your Grandma's sister and we wanted to pick us some blackberries. Well sir, Aunt Lizzie told us to put on boys' overalls—women didn't wear things like that in those days. There wasn't anybody around to see us and no menfolks about. It was a little dirt lane going up the hill where the blackberries grew, and cars hardly ever came along that bit of road. But, as luck would have it … "

Then she'd be on another subject or wandering off in her thoughts and the rest of that story didn't come along until I asked, days later,

"What happened that time you went berry picking with your sisters and wore overalls?"

She was baking biscuits, had her hands all in flour and her Carnation cream can with the top burned off sitting there to cut them out. She stopped with her hand in mid-air. And there was that Cheshire/Muttley laugh again, a sound like a motor trying to start, half whisper, half wheeze. She put the biscuits in the bread pan and turned them over in melted lard to coat both sides and stuck them in the oven of the wood cookstove.

Then she said, "Well, as luck would have it, along came a truck. And there we were, all three of us, and our cousin, too, and all of us dressed disgraceful in those boys' overalls. We'd of never lived it down. We heard the truck coming and we just tucked our hair under our hats and turned our backs to the road. Would have been all right, too, but Lorena started hollering, 'We're boys! We're boys! We're boys!'"

Most of Mom's stories were of hardship, but she told them humorously. It was humorous that she and Dad and my older siblings moved so far back that she and the two oldest boys had to use the handcar on the tracks to take them to the end of the spur, and then they had to climb down the side of a hill to get home, and pull themselves up again by holding to trees and roots to get back out of there.

It was humorous that they moved into a shack of a place one time and painted the whole inside of it with ugly green paint they'd been given, painting every wall in just one day so it would be clean enough to stay in.

"Oh, we did get so tired. We painted and we scrubbed and I had those floors shining—wore out linoleum on them, but it was clean. We pounded flattened-out tomato paste cans and covered up holes in the walls. Then we worshed up the best we could and made our beds on the floor and we were set for a good sleep. But about the middle of the night, one of the kids felt something crawling on him and he let out a yell and then we were all awake and we got up, lit the lamp and that whole place was crawling. Roaches everywhere—and they had little bitty green stripes. We'd spent our day a'painting roaches."

It was humorous that the young bride who'd never been around a drinking man thought her new husband was dead and went running to the neighbor for help, only to be told, "Oh honey, he's only went skidded. He'll come to, d'rectly."

It was humorous that she cooked the last food in the house, the last potatoes, to feed my older siblings, thinking for the next day, *something will turn up,* and when nothing did, getting the peelings from where she'd tossed them and washing them and cooking them to make potato skin soup.

There were stories about going on the hunt of the old man when he'd had too much to drink; about the time he climbed the telephone pole and sat up there and laughed at the cops who couldn't get to him. About the time he climbed the side of a building when the town was on fire and saved people trapped on the third floor and how they pulled the men out of the burning jail. And the time he walked into the church while a service was going on and called the preacher a liar *with a big oath to it.* She didn't use language, so when she had to tell about someone who did, that's what she'd say, *with a big oath to it.*

One year, my classmates and I were given the assignment to interview one parent about an event that changed their lives and Mom told me about Aunt Lizzie coming for her when she was sixteen to take her to live with her in Michigan and send her to secretarial school.

"I hadn't ever been anywhere. I had never ridden a train, hadn't ever been in a restaurant. We were about to order breakfast and I didn't have a clue how to go about it. Us kids always had oatmeal every morning. But here I was, all dressed up and the waitress ready to get me anything I wanted. Anything at all that I wanted! All of a sudden, I didn't know what to say. Finally, I just motioned to Aunt Lizzie and said, 'I'll have what she's having.' And the waitress brought us both a bowl of oatmeal."

Aunt Lizzie bought her niece new clothes and got her enrolled in classes. Then a telegram came that Grandma had been diagnosed with tuberculosis and Mom was needed back at home, and that quick, her life changed—or more to the point, didn't.

One of Mom's fondest memories was the time she got to go to Branson, Missouri with the church, along with the preacher's family, to an old time camp meeting. Her voice changed just a little when she spoke of it. It was a moment lifted out of reality. But reality caught up with her when she married the preacher's son.

"If I was ever to write my life," Mom said, "I'd have to write it as fiction, for there's no one would believe it as fact." She had always thought she'd grow up to be a missionary and she thought that's what life would be when the preacher's son started asking her out. She soon got her first clue it wasn't quite as she thought.

"He was dating this other woman right about the same time he was seeing me," she said, "and we found out about each other and we got in a big old fight over him. Still not sure who won."

She had a recurring dream all through her life that came back to her just a few months before she died, only with a different ending. In the dream, she had dropped her Bible in the well and she could see it down in the still water, far below her, and she kept trying to find someone to get it for her. She had that dream the first time when she was ten years old.

"Seems like that's the dream I'd have when things were … well, not going so well," she told me one of the last times I saw her. "But when I dreamed it the other night, it didn't turn out the same. I saw the Bible down in the well, just like before, but this time, somebody—I couldn't see who—told me, 'Nobody else can get the word for you. You got to do it yourself.' And I reached down and it was right there—and I picked up my Bible just as easy as you please."

In loving memory of Olivia Grace (Hall) Peek. b. Tuesday, March 21, 1911 d. October 17, 1989

Kate Dooley's heartfelt description of her mother gives us the portrait of a woman whose persistence and strength, in a time when women were not expected to have such qualities, held up her world. Her example represents the power in us all.

— SUE BOOTH-FORBES, Director, Anam Cara Writer's and Artist's Retreat

I Loved You Before

MARY IMO-STIKE

I loved you before I knew you,
when I was the chubby girl,
watchful and aware of all the ways I failed.
I looked for words
for all my feelings of alone.

Bound in the scratchy burgundy wool coat
with covered buttons to my chin
my perm-fried hair was pushed under
a fluffy, crème colored tam.
It was a sunny November day,
I posed for a Christmas card photo
among the prickly needles
of a piney shrub in Highland Park.

You told me
to explore the objects of wonder
stacked around Daddy's basement workbench:
cigar boxes containing small brass tacks and brads
the red, gold and leaf green tin box shaped like a tiny treasure chest
that held a cache of .22 rounds;
a surveyor's compass in a worn hard leather pouch,

a wood cod fish box with a sliding cover
full of cat's eye marbles.

Because you were in me
the woman I would be,
you saved me, took me out of church pews
placed your cool, calm palm
against my blushing cheeks,
let me know I could believe
in my hopes of climbing high in trees,
fly the way I longed for,
have pretty hair
and run as fast as boys.
You told me this prison I was stuck in
did not matter,
that this would pass.

We would escape,
it was not for life.

Mary's poem is striking to me for its subject matter because of the current generation of children growing up in homes where their parents are emotionally absent or even abusive because of the epidemic of drug addiction. What the poem's narrator leaves unsaid is that somebody loved her enough to make her, unknowingly, love her future self, that woman she'd not yet met. Without the earlier love from a parent or surrogate parent, her future self would have been someone she couldn't love, someone who would have had to stay in that youthful prison. I especially like the understated way that the poem implies that, though the narrator remembers feeling uncomfortable and alone, she was loved by a parent or other caregiver—the tam, the coat all buttoned up, the photo being taken, even the frizzy hair, speak of care being given (and while the fried hair showed someone wanted to change her looks, that was commonplace—the mothers of almost every straight-haired girl I knew when I was little, including me, made us suffer the horrible ammonia smell and those tight curler rods). Somebody wanted her to be warm, accepted, and admired. Mary's poem makes me wish such good luck to all children.

— EDWINA PENDARVIS, Author of *Ghost Dance Poems*

How I Became a Mother Naturally

JUDITH RAMSEY SOUTHARD

|||||||||||||||||||||||||||||||||||||||||||||||||||||||||||||||||||||||||||||||||||||||||

"Then while I was in that terrible pain, they gave me a shot that burned worse than anything I ever felt in my life. It was unbearable." My Aunt Katherine, who with her dark wavy hair always reminded me of Liz Taylor, was married to my mother's baby brother John. She had delivered her sixth child a few days before and was sharing the details with my mother and me. I am sure my mother regretted that her nine-year-old daughter was sitting there all agog listening to every gory detail of the horrendous torture my aunt had endured. As my Aunt Katherine paused to take a drag on her cigarette, my mother whispered toward me.

"It's not that bad. There's nothing unbearable." Fortunately, that is the part I remembered. My mother had gone through labor four times, and although I knew she had had to climb an icy hill to Sacred Heart Hospital in Richwood, West Virginia, on a frigid, snowy afternoon in January to deliver me, she had never mentioned unbearable pain. I decided that day that I was going to be like my mother—nothing unbearable or even bad. So, when I find myself in a group of women who have had birthing experiences they want to share, and we divide up into sides of the most horrendous, heinous deliveries and the easiest, most bearable, I always side with the latter.

Ray and I were married on Christmas Day 1970. Our wedding was so unplanned that he had to pull his cousin who was Monongalia County Clerk away from his turkey to go to the court house and prepare us a license. His mother showed her enthusiasm by finding a Methodist minister to perform the ceremony. My best friend Mary Lou, who lived on a farm near Morgantown, was willing to be a witness. I don't remember who arranged to use the Catholic Chapel of the Ecumenical

Student Union, but there we were at 4:30 Christmas evening, me in my favorite burgundy mini-dress and Ray in his only sport coat standing before the minister who stood with his back to beautiful stained-glass pictures of Christ on the cross and the Virgin Mary. Mary Lou stood beside me, and Ray's dad stood by him while his mother stood behind us. My parents lived in Elkhart, Indiana, so there was no way they could get there with the two hours' notice we gave them. That was the only year in recorded history that Mingo County teachers had to be back in the classroom three days after Christmas, so we spent our honeymoon on the road to Matewan where I taught eleventh grade English.

In Morgantown a month later, I became pregnant on a visit to Ray who was finishing his degree in Recreation and Park Management, which had been interrupted by the Vietnam War. What might seem like an abysmal lack of planning to an observer, turned out to be one of the most fortuitous days of my life. Although I was suspicious of my symptoms, I found out for sure when I visited the gynecologist in Williamson with whom I had made an appointment a few weeks earlier to get birth control pills. He assured me that I would not need them for seven or eight months and meanwhile I should come and visit him monthly. While Ray finished his degree at WVU, I taught eleventh graders in Matewan and grew a baby.

At the end of the school year, Ray and I moved into a tiny two-room and bath, furnished basement apartment with steep stairs leading to Grant Avenue in the Sunnyside area of Morgantown. Our landlady lived in the upper two floors of the house and appeared to be too elderly to navigate the stairs down to or up from our apartment. The windows in our bedroom/living room overlooked University Avenue on its way to the Evansdale Campus. The outside stairs from Grant Avenue led to a miniscule porch with a door into our kitchen. It was a good-sized kitchen with the best piece of furniture in the apartment, an antique Hoosier cabinet with a flour sifter and a sugar bin. Leading to the right out of the kitchen was a small hallway with a tiny closet into which my mother-in-law squeezed everything my husband had left in their house across town on Madigan Avenue with an overflow into the hallway, allowing only a narrow path to the bathroom with its toilet and claw foot tub. A door to the left of the kitchen led into the other room of the apartment which doubled as a sitting room and sleeping room.

I loved living in Morgantown that summer. Ray got a job through his parents' Republican connections as an engineer on Interstate 79, which was being laid through Monongalia County in 1971. He had sold my '67 Ford Mustang to his friend Mike, so without transportation on most days, I hiked the seven or eight blocks to the fabulous Morgantown City Library, where I found plenty to read. Consequently, even in my ninth month of pregnancy, my muscles were firm, although I was gaining more weight than my doctors liked. They didn't know the whole story. In Morgantown, I signed up with the Residents' Clinic connected with University Hospital. The visits were only two dollars, and the delivery turned out to be free. I was five months pregnant by that time, but they never asked if I had been seeing a doctor anywhere else, so I did not share that information with them. As a result, they did not have my medical records and did not know that I had already gained over thirty pounds.

I read "The Aesthetics of Childbirth" by Lindsy Van Gelder in the May 1971 *Ramparts Magazine*. I rebelled in my youth by leaning left and becoming a Socialist in my enthusiasm against the Vietnam War. *Ramparts* was the magazine of the movement and all things progressive at that time. In this article, Van Gelder described her daughter's birth using the Lamaze method. I could not afford, nor did I even know where to find the books that she listed with the details of how to do the Lamaze. There probably was a class going on in Morgantown at that time that Ray and I could have attended. For some reason, just from reading the description of Van Gelder's birthing experience, I thought I could do it. It did not bother me that her doctors and husband were also trained in the method. I did not even mention it to my husband. My doctors, not yet experienced, were just learning the "old school" and were considered progressive because they used the "saddle block."

I felt totally equipped with all the knowledge I needed to go in to that labor room and do natural without anybody's help.

When my contractions began on a Wednesday evening at dinner, it did not concern me that it was my husband's bowling night and his friends had planned to pick him up after dinner since he had totaled our only remaining vehicle a week earlier. I assured him that I would be fine and encouraged him to go ahead and bowl. It did not take much encouragement to make him feel okay about going and leaving me to labor alone. Looking back on it I wonder what we were thinking. This must be an example of "Ignorance is bliss." I felt so knowledgeable that I thought the right thing to do was to stay at home and pack my suitcase for the hospital. First, I drank a glass of red wine. I have no idea why. It didn't seem to hurt, but I would not recommend it. After that I got my nighties out, sewed a few missing buttons on, ironed them, folded them with some underwear and put them in a small suitcase.

I was reading Barbara Tuchman's *Stillwell and the American Experience in China,* borrowed from the wonderful library, but that evening I was having trouble concentrating on reading as my contractions were continuing to occur about five to 10 minutes apart. They were nothing more than uncomfortable, but I was beginning to think that perhaps they were not Braxton-Hicks which we called "false labor" at that time. Something that I had been sure I would have, and, based on the *Ramparts* article, I was determined not to go running in panic to the hospital.

I called Mary Lou, who was still living with her father on the family farm five miles out of Morgantown near Maidsville. Fortunately, she was at home and willing to spend some time on the phone. I told her my situation, and, to my surprise, she took it more seriously than I did. Apparently, she had not read the article in *Ramparts.* She became increasingly concerned and made me promise to call an ambulance if I began to feel at all like things were getting out of control. After talking to Mary Lou, I was energized to straighten the apartment and wash up the supper dishes. I felt ready to go to the hospital, but the contractions were still five to ten minutes apart and it was only around ten in the evening. I did not expect Ray home from bowling until at least midnight. I settled down on the bed on my left side, my only hope for comfort since the baby seemed to like kicking my bladder if I tried to lie on my right side. I opened the book on China and looked at it until Ray arrived home at midnight.

Here I am forty-seven years later writing about that night, but I cannot recall anything Ray talked about except that he had bowled one or maybe two turkeys. I was not familiar with bowling terms, but I did hope it was not something I would have to cook. He went to bed almost immediately with a warning from me that sometime during the night I would need him to call a cab to take us to the hospital.

It might seem strange that he was not more excited and insistent on doing something, but it was a blessing not to have to deal with any kind of advice from him at that moment. He went to bed and was asleep within minutes, although every light in our tiny apartment was on. I continued to try to get comfortable enough to read or sleep, but to no avail. Around three in the morning, I decided to take a warm bath and get ready to go to the hospital. It was during my bath that I noticed some blood in the water and wondered if I had perhaps waited too long. I got out of the tub, dressed for the hospital, woke Ray, and told him to call a cab. I was not satisfied with his speed in calling the cab (suddenly I was in a hurry), so I called the cab and rushed Ray through getting dressed. I followed him up the stairs from our apartment to the street where the cab was waiting.

Checking in to the maternity area of the hospital was easy. I felt good, and especially checking in early that morning as an uninsured patient with very little money, I was happy to be part of the Residents' Clinic. I went through all the pre-delivery routine feeling excited but not panicked. Just as I had expected from the birthing information in my *Ramparts*, my contractions stopped, and they put me to bed.

The resident on call was Doctor Steven Feaster, Mr. Mountaineer a few years before when we had graduated from WVU. The fact that upon examining me, he commented matter-of-factly, "Mrs. Southard, you know you are going to have twins," did not bother me at all since I was already of the opinion that I knew more than he did. I simply leaned back and outlined the one baby's position from her head to her feet on my stomach.

Things (the baby) started moving along quickly after my water broke. "Get the doctor; the baby's coming," I screamed at my husband who was the only other person in the labor room. Ray panicked and ran out of the room screaming for the doctor before he was needed. The *Ramparts* article had not explained about pushing, so after that the doctor, seeing Ray's level of stress, would not let him back into the room. I knew he was just outside the door because I could hear him talking and talking and talking. It was not comforting. He was not talking about me. I looked around the bare, utilitarian, off-yellow labor room. Between contractions, I was bored seeing an occasional taciturn nurse and hearing only my husband droning on to his newfound best friend in the waiting room.

I had carefully read the article in *Ramparts* many times, but it had not told me how to ask questions during labor. Consequently, I had no idea what was going on or what would be next. After an hour or so of contractions, a tall, blond young man with glasses whom I had seen several times in the Residents' Clinic, took me to another room and gave me an epidural. I was disappointed because until then it had been perhaps not exactly Lamaze but natural. However, I couldn't work up the courage to refuse the injection and demand to feel the rest of the pain since by then it was pain but not unbearable. I was relieved to discover that I only missed one contraction—the last one, and as if by magic, the doctor was standing there to catch the baby, and the clock on the wall to my right said 7:30. I felt a shudder, but no pain. A nurse who had suddenly appeared was holding a baby and took it off to the side out of my sight. She seemed to just shove it onto some shelf. I found my voice enough to say, "I want to see my baby." They showed me my baby girl for an instant. I saw the little bit of red peach fuzz on her head, her pretty little face so perfectly formed, and all her tiny fingers and toes. I can't say that I fell in love at that moment because I had loved her for months. It was she who had made this whole ordeal seem like some really great Christmas. After they took her away, I lay there watching the clock while the doctor stitched me up. It seemed to take a long time and the next day I discovered I had enough stitches to merit a field trip by the entire freshman medical class.

Later that day, I enjoyed the apprehensive look that passed between my mother and father-in-law when I bragged, "No unbearable pain, I could do this again next year."

In this delightful essay, Judith Southard shows us, through her own experience, that the pain of childbirth is all a matter of perspective. Through her vivid memories, she reveals that youthful impetuousness, abundant love, a bit of faith, and a bit of moxie are all you need to prepare to become a parent.

— SHEILA MCENTEE, Writer, Editor, Musician

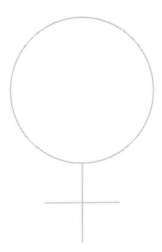

Daughter

RAJIA HASSIB

The thought first pops up in the middle of one of your sleepless nights: you never taught her to ride a bike. She is leaving for college in just over four months, and you never taught her to ride a bike. You toss and turn for the rest of the night, obsessing over that most recent one of your many failures: what if her friends all go riding and she can't join them? What if they make fun of her? In the morning you are groggy, your eyes puffy and your head throbbing. You wake up late from that last bit of sleep, and, by then, she has already left for school. You take your cereal to the kitchen window and eat while standing, watching the squirrels.

You wake her up too early the next Saturday, and she wrinkles her nose against the morning light seeping in through the blinds you just pulled open. It's the same expression she used to make whenever you woke her up as a child, before she started setting her alarm clock and getting up on her own, and you smile at that thought and at yourself for thinking of her childhood as gone, seeing her as the adult she believes she is. She pulls the covers over her head and mumbles something you can't understand. You nudge her, tell her to get up, promise her a day of adventure. You never give her adventure—only food, shelter, fussing over grades too close to an A but not close enough, a shoulder for her to cry on, a shoulder that, recently, she has stopped needing. She looks up at you with a quizzical expression on her face, then sits up in bed and shrugs, which you take as teenage speak for *whatever.* She is too polite to say that out loud to your face. That, at least, is a minor triumph.

You have borrowed a bike from a friend who has a college age daughter who knows how to ride bikes because, unlike you, your friend has always been put together and has checked off every skill she needed to teach her child before sending her out into the world. The bike is strapped to the back of the SUV, and your daughter stands with a coffee cup in her hand and looks at it before asking if she can drive. You're afraid to let her drive with the bike strapped to the car, and even though you've never driven with such a cargo, you still think that it would be safer if you do it. You don't tell her that. You just say you'd rather take the wheel, and she gets into the passenger seat. On the way to the parking lot of the nearby campus, she is on her phone, texting friends. You drive through the hilly West Virginia roads. You hope that the campus has poor cell phone reception, but you imagine it probably doesn't.

The bike is a bit too big for her. Her toes barely reach the ground. She has inherited your short stature—another failure of yours, another thing you feel the need to apologize to her for. She complains that the helmet straps cut into her neck, so you help her loosen them up just enough so that they don't hurt her but explain that they must be tight enough to keep the helmet in place, in case she falls. You hold on to the back of the seat with one hand and to one side of the handlebar with the other, tell her to pedal, then run next to her, letting go of the handlebar but not the seat, trying to keep her from falling. She is way too heavy for you to keep control of the bike with one hand—way too old, you tell yourself, because you should have done that when she was seven, not seventeen. Both of you manage only a few yards before the bike treacherously tilts to one side and she has to shoot one foot to the ground to keep from falling. Every time you stop, you help her get off the bike, push it to one end of the parking lot, get back on, and try again. It's Spring Break, and the campus is abandoned, which you know is one reason she has agreed to do this—no witnesses. After half an hour of starts and stops you are panting—even the short run next to the bike is killing you, and she is tearing up. She says she has no balance. She says she will never learn, that she doesn't really care, that no one rides bikes anymore anyway. You're startled by this, afraid that it is one more thing that you know nothing of, this lack of bike riding among American teenagers. They always seemed to do it in the movies you watched growing up half the world away, where you got to ride bikes only on summer vacation in beach resorts. You tell her that she can do it, that she does have balance, that it just takes some patience, that once she gets it she will know how to do it for life. She gets back on, tries again, and you switch to her other side, holding the back of the seat with the arm that is not cramping.

In the car ride back home, you are silent, and she is furiously texting. She texts with the thumbs of both hands, not with one forefinger, like you do, and you imagine all the things she is sharing with her friends, all the complaints she has about the ways you have failed her. You tell yourself that you should have listened to your husband and bought training wheels and attached them to the bike. You are thinking about whether you should tell her about the training wheels or wait till they arrive in the mail—you suspect she will refuse, if given a choice—when she screams at you to stop. You press on the brakes so violently that you both lurch forward, and the helmet that has been lying loose in the trunk shoots up and hits the back of the rear seat with a loud clang. Your heart is racing—did you hit something? Someone? She opens her door and jumps out, walks a few yards back, and leans down. You pull over to the side and join her. At the edge of the road lies a fawn, a baby, maybe only a few weeks old. You cannot understand how you didn't see it; it is lying right there, and you must have missed hitting it by only a few inches. It is injured—you see a splash of blood on its soft brown hide, a circular red dot among the many cream ones, a leg that is bent at a disturbing angle. You imagine another driver hitting it moments before, another person too preoccupied with her own thoughts to watch the road. You lean closer to touch it and your daughter yells at you not to do it, grabs your arm and pulls it back, tells you that if you touched it, you would imprint it with your own scent and its mother may not recognize it again and may abandon it. You cannot imagine a mother abandoning her daughter, ever, and you look around for that failure of a mother who has left her daughter, bleeding, at the side of the road, feeling both angry and sorry for her, judging her and wanting to hold her in a commiserating hug, to whisper that all mothers fail to a certain extent and that she shouldn't be too harsh on herself, but you see no does anywhere.

You don't know what to do next. Your instinct is to comfort the injured animal, but you grew up in a strip of a city between the desert and the sea, and you know nothing of deer. Your daughter does. Your West Virginian daughter knows things you don't know, it suddenly dawns on you, including, apparently, the phone number of a boy whose mother is a vet. She is already talking to the boy on the phone and asking if his mother can come look at the deer. It's a short, business-like conversation, and you resist an urge to ask her who the boy is and why she has never mentioned him to you. She hangs up and walks to the SUV, opens the trunk, and pulls out the emergency warning triangle that you keep there. She sets it up a few yards away from the fawn and then stands by it with her back to you, waving traffic away from the injured animal. You wait next to her, shifting from leg to leg, whisper something about how you could do that so that she is not standing in the middle of the road, but she says she can handle it. You look around—it's a residential road, right after a corner, so people will likely not speed through here. You deem the situation safe enough. You walk back to your car and stand with your back resting against the trunk, watching your daughter direct traffic.

The boy's mother comes equipped with a large blanket and a cardboard box. She leans down next to the fawn, looks at it without touching it, and you look at her son. He must be your daughter's age, but he is close to six feet tall and looks like a young man, not like the child you hoped he was, and when you look back at your daughter you realize that she, too, looks like a young woman. She is talking to her friend while watching his mother put gloves on and gingerly touch the fawn. You decide that the boy is just a friend, not a boyfriend. You think you still know your daughter enough to be able to tell by the way she stands with her feet apart, her arms crossed, giving more attention to the fawn than to the boy. When his mother announces that the fawn needs to be taken to her clinic, he helps her wrap it up in the blanket before lifting it into the cardboard box. The fawn kicks a leg but then surrenders, remaining quiet as they gently place it into its snug, protective carrier. Your daughter turns to you then and lets you know she will ride with them to the clinic. The boy says he will drop her off once they are done. His mother, apparently only now noticing you, takes her gloves off and walks up to you, shakes your hand, introduces herself. You shake her hand, mumble an introduction and a thank you. You watch her get in the car, watch your daughter climb into the back. You imagine she spends the trip looking over the backseat and at the fawn, but you can't see her through the opaque windshield.

You drop the bike off at your friend's on your way home. She says you can keep it, but you refuse, lie, tell her your daughter is already riding like a pro and won't need it. You're not used to lying, so you accent your lie by a nervous laugh, claiming that your daughter must have learned to ride while out with friends at some point in her childhood, or that perhaps your husband had taught her and you just forgot about it. On your way home, you drive through the hills you've lived among for close to twenty years, the landscape so different from the flat, open one you grew up in, and you try to not think of the countless things you have not taught your daughter because you don't know them yourself, things like how to tend to an injured deer.

That evening, she walks into your bedroom as you fold laundry and sits on the edge of the bed. She watches you while you work, but you don't look at her. You have spent the day wallowing in the many ways you have failed her, the many things you could have done better, and you suspect that she will be spending the next years thinking of all those same things, perhaps writing about them in college essays titled *My Mother's Shortcomings.* You cannot bear the thought of your little girl judging you or, worse, being disappointed in you, and you are equally terrified of the young woman now sitting on your bed, the one who knows things you haven't taught her, who has friends you have never heard of, who can flip out a phone and call just the right person for the job, who is comfortable standing in the way of incoming traffic, who is about to start a life you will be only marginally involved in, standing at the sidelines holding your breath, hoping she never gets hurt, never skins a knee or a heart, never suffers. You are so scared you start to tear up, and your daughter, your beautiful, young but not really so young anymore daughter, gets up and gives you a hug. She tells you she enjoyed spending the morning with you. She says that maybe next weekend you could borrow the bike and try again. You nod, say *sure,* know it won't happen, but keep on holding on to her, notice, again, that she is actually a bit taller than you are, lean your head onto her shoulder, and you wonder when this happens, this shift that turns the child into the comforting adult, how early it starts, when it has started and how you have missed it, and when she learned to do this, to care for injured fawns and injured mothers, to calm and comfort, and if, perhaps, you did teach her something after all, if you can claim some credit for the strength of her hug, the tender authority of her voice, the fact that she is carving her own path, and if any of that really matters, or if all that matters is that you have a daughter who is now an adult and who is standing there, hugging you, anchoring you in place even as she gets ready to fly.

|||

Rajia Hassib has written a poignant story about parenthood and the delicate balance between holding on and letting go. For all the character's worry about failing as a mother, the intimacy shared at the end of the story between mother and daughter demonstrates a profound success.

— SHARI HEYWOOD, Teacher

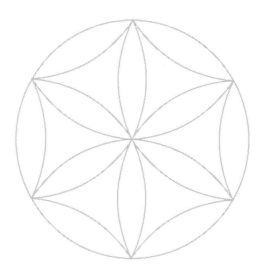

Lake of Fire

KAREN WORKMAN

The evening sun was blinding as I drove home on my usual route from work. Only today wasn't usual. My life as I knew it was collapsing and I was the one initiating the demise. From the outside looking in, I had it all together—perfect house, perfect career, perfect family, perfect life. My life thus far had been spent striving for perfection—academically, morally, religiously, physically—and I was good at it, really good. So why was I so unhappy? Why wasn't it enough? Why did I feel like I could spontaneously combust at any moment? I didn't know! What I did know is that I was drowning, going under for the last time, and no one was going to save me but me. But saving me meant choosing to step out of a life that was accomplished, comfortable, and safe. It meant admitting to those in my world that what they knew of me was not necessarily who I really was: Would they think I'm a fraud? Would they think I'm crazy? Would I lose my professional credibility that I'd worked so hard to build? And what about my son? He was an innocent child. What right did I have to tear his world apart? How selfish and self-centered of me to consider it. Maybe I was crazy.

Coming to this point of reckoning in my late thirties was not the way it was supposed to be. How did I get there? How was I to get out? I was a "holler girl" from rural West Virginia. I grew up with parents who loved me and a family that was stable. The small country church that my grandfathers helped to build was a central focal point of our lives. Church on Sunday mornings and evenings. Youth meetings on Monday nights. Prayer meeting on Wednesday evening and other church activities in between. I learned about God, love, heaven, and angels. Church was also the place that shaped my early views of what it meant to burn. Burning meant Satan, sin, and the everlasting lake of fire—where sinners go when they die if they don't repent and get "saved."

Fear is a powerful motivator, especially when the choice is being an outcast and spending eternity burning in hell or being loved and living forever in heaven. Seemed like a no-brainer to me. So my soul was "saved" from burning in hell at the tender age of six by my public profession of faith that Jesus was my savior. In this denomination's teachings, being "saved" once wasn't good enough; you could always backslide and find yourself facing the potential for eternal burning yet again. I was determined that would never happen to me. So I became THE perfect Christian girl—never drank, never smoked, never cursed, taught Sunday School, sang in the choir, led the youth group. And lest there be any doubt that I could achieve perfection, I remained a virgin until marriage. All good qualities. But being the perfect Christian girl, at least in that world, also meant sacrificing my own needs to serve others first, not displaying anger, accepting without question church teachings, and not associating myself with sinners. What I didn't know then is that suppressing needs, desires, and my own voice stoked a fire inside of me that was smoldering. In my mind, the more I was able to be that perfect Christian girl, surely the more I'll be loved, I'll avoid hell and the outcome should be joy and happiness. Right? My standards for myself were very high and failure meant losing my immortal soul. From age six to my late thirties, my decisions in my personal and professional life were filtered through this somewhat twisted lens of morality and religiosity. And the embers burned.

My quest for perfection extended beyond protecting my immortal soul. School lessons and studying came naturally to me. I enjoyed learning. I enjoyed the competition to be the "best in the class." I liked the approval from my teachers. One day in elementary school my second-grade teacher, Mrs. Fleming, asked what we wanted to be when we grew up. Responses from the class fell along some typical gender lines—boys wanted to be coal miners, firemen, police officers. Girls wanted to be mothers, nurses, teachers. When it was my turn, I said "I want to go to college, get my Master's degree and own a business." To this day I don't know where that response came from. Not too many holler girls had that as a dream. And so I set out to be the perfect student. I made straight A's in elementary, middle and high school. I was in the Honor Society, class president, all county band, head majorette. I earned my Bachelor of Science degree in Computer Science and went on to complete a Master's degree in Business Administration with A's in every class. The accomplishment felt good. And yet, the fire inside was still smoldering. I found technical subjects such as science and math to be comforting—they were logical, analytical and there was a "right" answer or solution at some point. That method of thinking also distracted me from the burn. I didn't have to feel it, acknowledge it, or explore it. I could ignore it.

Success in academics didn't necessarily translate to success with boys. I didn't date much, if at all, in high school. Being a "perfect" Christian girl meant I needed to find a "perfect" Christian boy—or as close to one as I could. Finding one, or one finding me was not an easy task. My church congregation was less than 100 with not many young people. My father was a Deputy Sheriff in the county, which didn't necessarily play out in my dating favor. I also observed that being known as the "smart girl" in school and being attractive didn't easily co-exist. You were one or the other. I chose being "smart." The one dating relationship that I had in high school was squelched because he was Catholic. And in my religion, being Catholic didn't qualify as being Christian. Since nothing could ever come of that relationship, I broke it off. Smoldering, glowing, embers.

When I started college, I vowed that my dating life would be different. Others didn't know my academic past, my dad, or my church. The odds were greater that I could find someone that even if they weren't a "perfect" Christian yet, there was the potential to become one. And that's just what happened. It was more important to be "equally yoked," as the church would say, to be happy than to be true to what you feel. Or that was my interpretation. Those embers erupted into flames a couple of times when I tried to call off the wedding, but they were quickly doused when I was told that it was too late to back out and my duty was to go through with it. So, I graduated from college, got married, moved out of state, and started my first professional job within a 30-day time span. I was becoming good at ignoring myself. Outrun the burn. Drenched but not extinguished.

My professional life followed a similar script. I worked hard and long hours. Took on challenging roles. Enjoyed being recognized by others for my knowledge, skills, and abilities. Receiving professional accolades was seductive. Impacting others through the work that I was doing was rewarding and satisfying for me. Making a difference in how individuals saw themselves and others at work motivated me more than the money. I found that moving up the corporate ladder was relatively easy for me and it provided financial and social perks that I never thought would be in my reach as a holler girl. Pouring myself into my career for the sake of "a good life" for my family and me, while worthwhile, left little time for me to attend to the flames inside. I was good at what I was doing. I was being responsible and taking care of securing my future. I was exceeding expectations I had set for myself as well as others' expectations of me.

A decade passed. I accepted my role as a good Christian wife. I also declared I never wanted to have children and my husband seemed to be ok with that. I couldn't see myself as a mom, plus I enjoyed my work life too much. My husband and I were good roommates. Neither emotional and physical intimacy nor passion was part of the relationship. But isn't that what I had signed up for? I didn't need that anyhow. Just push the embers down. But the universe had other plans. I found out I was pregnant after 10 years of marriage. At the age of 33 I became a mom to beautiful baby boy. A colleague of mine, who also was a practicing Hindu, gave me these words of wisdom, "Western philosophy says that you have a child so that you can teach them something. Eastern philosophy says that you have child because you need to learn something." Those words struck my heart to the core and the relationship with my son made the embers grow and glow.

It was through my professional experiences that I started to realize that maybe there was a professional path where I could be more true to myself while at the same time earning a living. The opportunity to leap into running my own business presented itself and I closed my eyes and jumped. Was I nuts? I had a small child, big mortgage, benefits, 401K, good salary. A flame broke through. I had to do it. It was scary and exhilarating. I was the only one in control of my own professional destiny. I could choose to take on projects or choose to decline them. I could choose to work with a client or not. I could choose my colleagues. I could choose when I worked. Shedding the corporate expectations of me provided the freedom and the space for me to explore me, maybe for the first time in my life. What work was meaningful for me versus meaningful for others? What gives me energy versus depleting it? What masks have I been hiding behind all these years? What makes my soul sing? What example do I want to set for my son? Am I happy? Am I sad? Or am I just numb?

There are those moments in our lives when the universe conspires to slap us up the side of the head, otherwise known as wake-up calls. Mine came on a Saturday morning. My son's bedroom was upstairs over the master bedroom with a set of stairs leading to the hallway by my bedroom. I could hear him get up, come downstairs, pass by my bedroom and head to the basement where his dad was sleeping. This was his "normal" routine, to wake up daddy in the basement. And the flames exploded into a raging fire. I did not want this to be normal.

And so I made the choice to burn, really burn. For me, I had to fling myself into the crucible of fire. I had to sacrifice myself to the goddess within me. I had to burn to learn. The hell fire of religion became a personal internal fire of purification, of refinement. I realized that I was the one who could save me, no one else. And I was worth choosing to save. While contemplating my decisions, the destruction it would cause, I also had a vision for me, my life, my son's life and rebirth on the other side. I knew that I had to be totally spent, reduced to ashes in order to have a clearing where the real me could emerge, create and move forward. So I let the flames come, the glorious, hideous, redemptive and restorative burn. Through the fire I found me, my voice and my power of choice. I found joy, happiness, and peace. I learned that in order for someone else to love me just for me, I had to first love me just for me.

And a new fire burns within. I'm not afraid of the burn anymore. Now the fire is one of passion and confidence, of compassion and forgiveness, of love and creativity and of a ferocious commitment to never lose myself again. I am truly grateful for and LOVE my life. I remarried and have a husband who shows me daily what it means to be loved for just being me. We have a wonderful blended family that loves and supports each other. I consciously choose friends and work that fulfill me. And I am motivated more by what gives me energy than by what others may want for me. Life still presents challenges from time to time but somehow they never seem insurmountable anymore. So ask me, was it worth the burn? Hell yeah!

||||||||||||||||||||||||||||||||||||||||||||||||||||||||||||||||||||||||||||||||||||||||||||||||||||||||||||||||||||||||||||||||||||||||||||||||||||||||||||||||||||||||||||||||||||||||||||

Don't be surprised if Karen's account of going through the refiner's fire strikes a familiar chord. The particulars of her experience may differ from yours, but the challenge is the same: endure, transform, emerge, become.

— CARLA MCCLURE, Editor

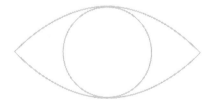

The Dream That Died

MAGIN LASOV GREGG

I'm massaging shampoo through my scalp when the light changes, turns sharp and thin and white. There's a clamping in my belly, the slightest pinch. I close my eyes. *I'm pregnant.* I think. I have no evidence to support this thought. Only the strongest intuition. *I'm pregnant.* I've had this kind of knowing one other time in my life, sixteen years ago, when I sat in my D.C. apartment and saw the living room walls turn salt-lamp pink. They swirled like water while I sat stock-still. When the pink turned back to white, when the walls stopped moving, I knew my mother had died. The light, the moving walls, had been her spirit shooting out from the earth, a great spark passing by me one last time.

In the shower, I know I'm pregnant the same way I'd known I'd lost my mother. There's a similar presence, a gentle, tender hovering. When the first pregnancy test I take issues a single blue subtraction line, my certainty does not fade. The next test, I know, will be plus-sign positive. A few days later, I'm not surprised when the blue symbol appears, faint as a whisper, *pregnant.* For the next few days, I'm ebullient and scared. Fear is the filmy layer sinking beneath my happiness, a negative image blistering in the sun. Nothing in my life has ever come easy. An inner voice I want to *shush* tells me this pregnancy won't stick.

I begin talk to myself when I'm driving in my car, running errands. At 36, I'm a community college professor, respectable. But a person looking in my car windows would see a woman sitting alone carrying on a conversation with no one. The ant-sized thing I'm talking to, the embryo inside of me, has not grown ears. But I believe he can hear me. I believe he's a *he.* When I squint, I can see him. He has my eyes, dark and deep-set. He has the sand-colored hair Carl had as a boy. The ends curl into ringlets. His mouth is Carl's mouth. His smile, too.

"I love you," I whisper, when I am alone. I pat my stomach, which is growing, filling with fluid. Most days, I eat giant hunks of watermelon while standing up at my kitchen counter. I'm gaining a pound a week. I bring a water bottle everywhere I go. No matter how much I drink, I want more.

One night, a colleague and I give a public lecture on *The Handmaid's Tale*. All night, I'm smug with joy because a baby secret swims deep inside of me. My belly rounds beneath the pink T-shirt I'm wearing, hints at a truth I can speak in six more weeks. But goose bumps prickle my legs even though it's July. I bundle up in blankets when I go to bed. Still, my teeth clang while I sip tea at the breakfast table. Blood comes next. A thin line on toilet tissue—a rust-colored subtraction sign.

Despite the fact that 20 percent of all pregnancies end in miscarriage, my Ob-Gyn practice, full of flyers for pregnancy classes and doulas, doesn't send me home with a "What to Expect" handout the day I start to bleed. Nor do I get a referral to a support group, or a list of mental health clinicians who specialize in pregnancy loss.

The clinicians I see treat me as healthy, because that is how I appear to them. But in these early days of loss, my brain fuzzes, turns woolen. Thoughts float past me, one-by-one, and I cannot grab hold. One afternoon, Carl drives me to the grocery store because we're out of food. I move in a daze down aisles that reek of dead fish.

On the one-week anniversary of our miscarriage, Carl calls for me to come into the basement. He needs help folding laundry. I'm on the second-to-last step, when our dog begins to bark. But I hear a baby's cry. Half my body rushes back up the stairs, the other half tilts toward Carl. A flip flop flies off my foot as I skid to the floor.

"Watch out," Carl yells. But he's too late. The warning means nothing. I've already fallen. My right foot makes contact with the concrete landing first.

Pain sparks through me when I try to stand. My foot turns purple, swells. I crawl up the stairs, hands-and-knees-style, the way I did when I played "babies" with my sister years ago. The dog waits for me, mouth agape. No more barking.

My broken foot is something I can post about on social media. I get more condolences for a visible injury than I ever do for my miscarriage. Friends turn up at my house with flowers and cards for the foot. I start the semester in a plastic orthopedic boot and keep my office door closed.

"I'm here. Please knock," I write on a sticky note, then tape it to the door.

And I am *here*, seated behind a desk where a statue of the Buddhist god Jizo assures me the loss I bear is real, even as I worry I have no right to claim this loss when I was barely pregnant. I am *here* in a department where all my female colleagues are mothers or stepmothers. I am *here* on a campus where a student brings his infant son to class on the two-month anniversary of my miscarriage, and everyone sits in awe of my ability to hush the baby while they write.

And I am *there*. Back on the bathroom floor the morning I start to bleed. I am on the examination table in my Ob-Gyn practice, where a midwife who looks like Sarah Palin refuses to tell me I'm losing my pregnancy because she doesn't "want to be wrong and look stupid." I'm in my sister's minivan, bleeding out my most dearly held dream, while her infant son cries, and I beg her to stop repeating the name I can't claim. *Mommy.*

"You've got to do something," a friend tells me one afternoon, while I sob until makeup melts off my face. "You're going to have a nervous breakdown."

But what can I do? I know how to mourn an actual person. How do I grieve a dream that died?

I leave campus early and drive into the Shenandoah Valley. In late autumn, land shrivels beside my car. Trees, shorn of leaves, tilt along the curving road. Dim hills huddle in the distance. I'm heading into those hills, to a Bed & Breakfast, where I'll immerse myself in the waters of a Japanese ritual bath. Once I enact this ritual, I'll be *okay*, restored. I weep as my car skirts deeper into the valley. This is my last good cry. Even as I think those words, I know I am lying.

Later, when I crawl into the ritual bath, I recall the *mikvah* I visited after my mother's death. In Jewish tradition, immersion in *mayyim hayyim*, living waters, signifies rebirth. Traditionally, women visit a *mikvah* after conversion, marriage, or menstruation. As a younger woman, I'd gone to the *mikvah* to mark losses I'd needed to transcend, to draw an imaginary line between before and after. This time, I'd chosen a non-Jewish space for my miscarriage ritual. Shame runs hot on my skin. I'd failed to do the one thing I'd been told to do since I was a girl: be fruitful, multiply, bear Jewish children.

"Ancient rabbis did not consider a child to be a child until it cried," my Hebrew school teachers told me in classrooms that smelled of paper and dust. They said a child was not a child until the eighth day, when circumcision was performed, or a name was given. By this logic, when I'd lost my pregnancy I'd lost no thing—nothing. And so, I have nothing to mourn. But I'm haunted by the memory of my last ultrasound, when I'd longed to see the spark of a heartbeat, and saw nothingness instead. As hope and fear flooded me, I recalled Adrienne Rich, who wrote of silence:

> It has a presence / It has a history a form / do not confuse it / with any kind of absence.

In the Japanese ritual bath, the absence of my unborn child weighs on me: heavy, relentless. I sink beneath pale water and whisper *goodbye*. My chest clenches as I say the word. I'm not ready to let go.

When my head rises above the water's surface, I notice condensation smearing patio windows that separate the bathhouse from a fallow field. Outside, deer forage beneath the season's first harvest moon. But I feel no renewal, only the sense of time moving on. I have no other choice but to do the same. I think of Carl, alone in our house, sad because I am sad. I will not return to him as the person I'd been before. That person is gone.

The next day, my car windshield blurs like water on the drive home. I pull over, close my eyes, and wait for the blurriness to pass. A migraine pulsates behind my right eye. My arms and legs tingle, as if insects crawl beneath the skin. When I walk from my car to a restaurant, my legs wobble. Will they give out too?

Weeks later, I sit on a white couch while a psychologist who takes no health insurance uses the perinatal grief scale to assess me. "Your resilience scores are high," she says, like this is a good thing. And it is, I suppose. Resilience offers a strand of hope in a world where all other hope has vanished. Resilience says the hopelessness and depression will slink away.

I don't need a grief scale to tell me I'm as sad as I was when I lost my mother. But I'm less sad than when every PhD program I applied to rejected me, dashing my dreams of becoming a Shakespeare scholar. Both losses pop into my head in the psychologist's office, as my eyes land on a set of candles near the couch. The candles kindle no flames. I consider lighting one. I want to watch smoke curdle, see wax drip into nothingness. A poem I've taught for the past decade comes back to me—Langston Hughes' "Harlem."

"What happens to a dream deferred?" the poem's first line asks.

My community college students have lived enough to know the pain of a dream that dries up, festers, or explodes. They've been abused, addicted, evicted, at war. One of the best answers a student ever gave to Hughes' question was a shrug.

"Sometimes what we want isn't what we need," she'd said. "Know what I mean?"

At the time, I didn't know what she meant. But I'm beginning to understand. I can no longer dismiss my medical symptoms as "aging."

My problems, I suspect, aren't mental. How can I care for a baby when I can't trust my legs to carry me, or when exhaustion nails me to the bed each morning? What kind of mother will I be? I don't make a follow-up appointment with the psychologist.

A few weeks later, I listen to a chakra-clearing meditation while I cook dinner. I like the melody of the meditation. The *ding* of the gong feels like a clearing. As I stir garlic into melted butter, I offer the closest thing to a prayer I can muster. Each cell of my body calls out for truth. *Whatever is wrong, I want to know.*

An itchy rash erupts on my shoulder that same night. When a doctor in an urgent care center diagnoses me with shingles, I weep on his table—I'm not used to doctors believing me. When the "shingles" rash migrates to the other shoulder, a new primary care physician orders a Lyme disease test, and I laugh at the suggestion. My rash is not a bull's eye. I have no memory of a tick bite.

"My daughter had Lyme and your rash looks just like hers," she replies, not cracking a smile.

Despite my initial disbelief, this doctor turns out to be right. The tests she orders are CDC conclusive. I'd had Lyme when pregnant and when I'd miscarried. I suspect I'd had it for at least five years, the furthest point where I can trace the onset of symptoms. Five years ago, I'd gone to the emergency room with uncontrollable vomiting and the worst headache of my life. I presented flu-like symptoms in the middle of July, but I never saw a doctor that night. Staff moved me into a hallway, far from other patients' line of sight. I'd fallen asleep there, then gone home after 1 a.m., when the vomiting and headache subsided.

"You probably just have a virus," a staff member had told me, and I believed her because I hadn't been hiking recently. I didn't know how Lyme could travel on the backs of mice into the suburban fields where I walked our dogs, didn't know how a poppy-seed sized tick could hitch onto a dog's foot, then attach to me.

These years, the years Lyme goes undetected in my body, these years are my childbearing years.

I am almost 37 when I begin treatment, which means swallowing 30 pills a day. Months go by, and I am still swallowing pills, but I begin to feel like the healthy woman I used to be, although she's a shadow-self. Each day promises recovery or threatens relapse.

Another July comes, and I'm well enough to travel to Puerto Rico. Each night, Carl and I walk a beach behind our hotel. We take pictures of our shadows on the sand. In a trick of light, they double, and I wish expanding our family could be as easy. The moon turns the water to gold.

One day, we snorkel a Caribbean reef, then swim the waters of Isla Icacos, an uninhabited island lush with white sand, palm trees, and crystalline tide pools. When we retreat to the beach to relax, I sit in the surf and let waves rock my shoulders. Each time water warms me, I sink deeper into the tide.

I recall an image of El Yunque National Forest, where clouds cloaked the mountain top. I'd visited the rainforest a few days prior. Our guide told us the Taino people believed the forest's cloud cover held divine secrets. El Yunque means "Forest of Clouds," and the word "secret" is implied by this name. To cloud is to keep hidden. *Claro*, the opposite of cloudy, means to make clear, to reveal. El Yunque is a forest of secrets precisely because it is a forest of clouds, a place to hide and to be hidden.

At Isla Icacos, I sit with a secret of my own. I'm too scared to say this secret out loud. More terrified of what this secret will say about me than the truth of the secret itself.

Had I not had my miscarriage, I'd have missed this magical swirl of sun, sea, sand.

I am not grateful for what I've lost. But I am grateful to be here, to feel healthier than I've felt in years, to be dazzled by a West Indies sun, to have another chance at life.

A few feet away, Carl sits on a blanket, shields his eyes with a book.

I don't know if we'll try again for a baby, and I hope we will, despite all the reasons why we shouldn't, all the risks, medication, and awful unknowns. I conjure the most hopeful image I can muster, an image to carry me through the uncertainty ahead. Our unborn child glimmers, smiles Carl's smile. As always, the child's eyes are mine. I close my eyes. He's gone as quickly as he arrived. On this day, I do not feel the usual pang of loss. I am releasing him the same way the shore releases water to the sea.

Sand sifts through my fingers. The granules fall back to the waves, and I whisper: *let go, let go, let go*. I'm talking to no one again, and I don't know what I'm relinquishing, a baby or a dream. But it feels good to unburden myself, to no longer cling to what escapes my grasp.

We each live our own grief, that most secret of inner realities, that shapes what we become, what we believe we can be. In this lyrical, gentle, yet bold essay, Magin LaSov Gregg explores love, loss, and illness, and sets them right where they always surface—amid the goings on of everyday life. She captures the fragility and beauty and hope of what it is to be human.

— MARCIA ROBERTS GREGORIO, Retired Teacher

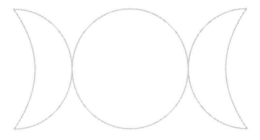

And with a Word, I Began

CANDACE JORDAN

"In the beginning was the word." It could be the first sentence of my autobiography. From the very beginning, I loved language. Those first words I heard—mother-music, the sounds that lulled me or set me yearning, the tones that taught me how to play—they've never really left me. My first spoken word? "Light." It illuminated the beginning of a lifetime flooded with words.

I was a military brat whose only real home was in my head. At age 4, I was a pair of red Texas cowboy boots with a British accent: a bit lost. But I found my magical match in fourth grade: Kathy Petersen—she of the purple velour bell-bottoms and the faerie face. Together, we wrote a novel: Johnny and Star: A Boy and His Horse. We were giddy with the discovery that we could create a *whole world* with words. *We* were in control! What would Johnny have for breakfast on the day he had to sell his horse? *We* got to decide! (We gave him blueberry pancakes to cheer him up. It was a sad day.) On the playground, instead of playing dodge ball or jumping rope, Kathy and I made up commercials, tossing words back and forth. "Tired of unwanted hugs from creepy guys? Try the new steel bra!"

The day in fifth grade when I checked *The Phantom Tollbooth* out of the school library was the day I finally realized just how word-smitten I was. The novel is stuffed with word play—A car that "goes without saying" (it only moves when you're quiet), a Spelling Bee who flies around the word market, upsetting crates of icy Is and crunchy Cs (yum!), an island called "Conclusions" that can only be reached by jumping. I saved every penny to buy my own copy, tears in my eyes as I bore it reverently to the checkout counter. When I got home, I immediately got my embossing labeler (very trendy in the 70s) and typed out "I love this book," along with my name, claiming it as my own. Because now I had learned that not only can you create worlds with words, but words have layers of use and meaning beyond the mundane.

Soon after, I discovered my dad's thesaurus. Could it be? This *treasure* in my very own home?! It wasn't long before I was amusing myself by rewriting classic nursery rhymes:

> *A trio of myopic rodents. A trio of myopic rodents.*
> *Note the manner in which they flee. Note the manner in which they flee.*
> *En masse, they pursued the agriculturalist's spouse,*
> *Who severed their caudal regions with a cutting implement,*
> *In the course of your lifespan, have you ever descried a similar*
> *phenomenon,*
> *As a trio of myopic rodents?*

(For me, this was very entertaining.)

I had a superpower: I had words other people didn't have. Where most people merely skimmed the top of the well of language, I fully submerged myself, in a kind of lyric baptism. One afternoon in my third decade, I visited Coopers Rock, a state forest near my home in West Virginia that features a stunning view of the Cheat River valley. Seeking solitude, I sat back in a corner of the platform, observing as person after person scaled the steps, saw the view and exclaimed, "Awesome!" It happened again. And again. It frustrated me so much that I began to fantasize about handing out thesauri to all visitors. How the beauty of the place was diminished by that lazy word! And so, I believe, was people's experience of that beauty. Couldn't they see that what they thought was an "awesome" view was really a verdant vista riotous with rhododendron bloom and old hemlock, soaring hawks attending the Cheat River on its golden progress through the valley? (OK, so I have a weakness for purple prose.)

Lilac. Icicle. Mellifluous. Aubergine. Gaelic. Aurora. Words taste of color and light. When I write well, the light shines from them. Through the long days, they comfort me. As I fall asleep, I intone a mineral lullaby: feldspar, galena, jasper, mica, chalcedony. I fight anxiety and insomnia with words. My severe anxiety requires a potent antidote. I quiet my inner trembling by solving crossword puzzles or playing "The Alphabet Game"—I pick a category (lakes, flowers, birds) and try to name one item for every letter of the alphabet. It's a soothing exercise. And spiritual guides have long known the power of a mantra to tame the beasts of the psyche! Mine is "calm." I use words for fight *and* flight. According to Margaret Atwood, "A word after a word after a word is power." I have found my writing ability to be a formidable tool in my environmental activism. And when I want to escape, there's Jabberwocky or Xanadu, Heathcliff's moors or Alice's looking glass. A multitude of word-made worlds, enough to last beyond a lifetime.

"You're a life support system for hair." My boyfriend at the time didn't particularly mean it as a compliment, but as he said it, I fell a little more in love with him. A friend from high school calls me his "fairygodfriend," thus winning my everlasting loyalty. Every man I've ever loved has wooed me with words. My partner and I flirted through wordplay. We would try to stump one another at the coffee shop. He won me at last with "crepuscular." I tamed him with "absquatulate." If you can turn a word on the lathe of wit, my heart will be drawn to you. Keep me around with the ties of metaphor and consonance, simile and synecdoche.

As I've gotten older, I've seen, more and more, the generative force of words. It's astonishing, really, how much your reality can change depending on which words you use to describe it. As Desmond Tutu remarked, "Language is very powerful. Language does not just describe reality. Language creates the reality it describes." Contained within one little word might be respect, dismissal, love, hatred, disrespect, surprise, confusion, and/or exasperation. Then there is the matter of tone. And that's where words on social media can really become confusing. There is no way, really, to communicate tone—other than by accompanying a statement with an emoji or by being extremely careful with context. I started a group on Facebook for women with DCIS, a type of cancer I had 10 years ago. We have about 3,000 members. Word choice is crucial to communicating in a group that large, without face-to-face cues. I have had to reprimand some women who, instead of using the words "mastectomy," "radiation," and "chemo" will use words like "slash," "burn," and "poison." Obviously that is not productive communication. I imagine someone about to have treatment or recovering from surgery reading those words, and the lack of empathy stuns me. Maybe it's just the disconnectedness of the medium. If they were face-to-face with a woman suffering, with bandages and tubes, would they still use such words unflinchingly?

Words foster empathy, and I attribute much of my high capacity for empathy to the books I have read in which diverse characters suffered and bled, fought and triumphed. There is nothing like Shakespeare for a lesson in human nature. And to know true heroism, you need only read *The Diary of Anne Frank*. I worry that in an age of texting and emojis, the potency of words will be lost—that amazing power they have to touch the heart directly. Gmail offers predictive responses that you can choose to answer various types of emails. We don't even have to come up with our own words and thoughts to communicate with friends, coworkers, and family anymore; Google will do it for us! And so our verbal intelligence is diminished.

I often refer to myself as a "fool for love." I allow myself to be vulnerable or silly in order to encourage others to open up and feel less alone. It is very conscious behavior on my part. To me, it is a form of activism and an act of courage. Several years ago, I started asking a "Question of the Day" on Facebook. I consciously use these carefully worded questions to attempt to enrich the lives of others on a daily basis. I'm trying to take people to a positive place—good memories, stimulating ideas. Often, people who respond will then connect with the responses of people they have never met, and a friendship may begin. All part of my evil plan!! I enjoy using the verbal part of my brain to put a little bit of a positive twist on the day. Since I have health issues that limit my ability to socialize regularly in person, I use my written words to make up for all the in-person hugs, silences, and conversations I might have otherwise.

The questions also help me process my thoughts and give me and my friends an opportunity to express ourselves in short, often poetic form— to lift our thoughts above the rush and the mundane, as in this question I posed several months ago: *"What, to you, is the essence of the feminine?"*

My response:

My first thought was to go with the school of Georgia O'Keeffe and say the flower, but when I thought more about it I decided that my answer is water. It has the capacity to flow and adapt its path in the face of obstacles; it is beautiful and healing. It nourishes, and yet its strength can be immeasurable. It gives birth. It softens hard edges. In the form of ice, it can be adamant and unyielding (as women can be when their children or loved ones are threatened). 'Course, I guess all of that could describe a man as well.

My friend Colleen's response:

Intuitiveness, and for me personally, a profound instinct, really a need to nurture and protect things that I love. Family, animals and the natural world around me.

In times when the news on our feeds is like a battering ram to our hopes, I try to create a safe, positive moment, as when I asked people to share a cozy memory from their childhood. My friend Terrie True's evocative response:

Sitting on my Nana's lap, listening to her describe, in the richly descriptive vocabulary of a fashion designer, the colors, textures, patterns and customs of Faeryland in layered detail. These were not faery "tales" but elaborate travelogues and anthropologies, histories and journals of one who had been there personally. Sometimes we each had our own beautiful and unique teacups with tea and milk and sugar; perhaps thinly sliced and buttered raisin toast with white icing. The chandelier in the dining room was dimly lit, casting shadows on the wallpaper, black with large brightly colored parrots. It was both comfortably familiar and utterly exotic ...

Throughout my life, descriptors have had immense power. How I describe events and circumstances to myself determines the tenor of my life and my self-concept. Thirty years ago, I began to experience sudden episodes of overwhelming fatigue, and times when—if I was afraid or angry or sad—my body simply shut down. For a long time, I wasn't able to function beyond doing the minimum a human must do to stay sentient. I tried to work, but every time I did, there would come a time when I would have to call off yet *another* day because I just didn't have any energy—or because I was afraid of having one of my "episodes" at work. I was also in the throes of deep, clinical depression. Finally, I applied for disability. With this assistance, I am able to work part-time and maintain a level of productivity that doesn't send me over the edge. But throughout that time, the doctors I saw were mostly psychiatrists, and although they did not come right out and say it, I knew many of them thought I was lazy and crazy. I had a script of that in my head after a while, and a burden of shame that has never completely left me. In 2002, I was diagnosed with narcolepsy. At that point I felt freed. I wasn't lazy or crazy! My brain just didn't work properly! My shame level went down greatly because now, instead of telling myself I am lazy, I can remind myself it's the narcolepsy. What a difference it has made to my quality of life! What a beautiful word: Narcolepsy. It freed me to have compassion for myself.

Because I am such a verbal person, my spirituality is inevitably bound up with words and language also. My native way of loving is through language. I am the queen of the love letter, and I regularly send postcards and letters to my friends to communicate my affection. In dire times, I believe God or the Universe helps me to think of the best words to say to a troubled friend. At those times, I feel like a language conduit, the words flowing through me like water.

My mother is a quiet one—the complete opposite of me. I bring her gifts of language in the hopes that she will open up her well of words and tell me all her deepest thoughts. At this point I accept the fact that we are just different, and that her squeezy hugs and her persistent concern for my needs are her way of communicating love. But when I was younger, I tried to woo her with my wit, writing her a series of playful love notes, such as this one:

> *Dear Mom,*
> *According to recent scientific research (published 1/09 in Science magazine), having a great mommy extends one's lifespan, enables one to do better at board games, fills one with a sense of well-being, heightens one's sense of fun, enables one to juggle small appliances, maximizes one's ability to do effective origami, and increases (by 38%) one's ability to interpret ancient Sumerian texts. Wow! I knew some of this stuff (from delightful experience), but I can't wait to put on my reading goggles and get to reading that Cuneiform script!*
> *Love you,*
> *Me*

Language has enlivened every aspect of my life and has truly empowered me throughout, helping me to rise above the shame and self-doubt that come in a culture where disability carries a stigma, delighting me even in the darkest times, allowing me to express my love in a way unique to me, creating space for me to grow as a human being. I feel so privileged to be a person who appreciates and cultivates what Dylan Thomas refers to as the "syllabic blood"—the expression of the heart's truth through words.

This is a lovely and touching tribute to the power and solace of words, as well as the fun they can provide. And thank you for a new word game. My first category is going to be Amazing Women Writers.

— **BELINDA ANDERSON**, Author of *Jackson vs. Witchy Wanda: Making Kid Soup*

A Suite of Three Poems

LAURA TREACY BENTLEY

||||||||||||||||||||||||||||||||||||||||||||||||||||||||||||||||||||||||||||||

Imagine an Aging Miss Emily

basking on a beach towel
with the cupola windows
opened wide to summer's sun.

She's working on her tan,
nibbling at gingerbread,
and sipping Long Island Iced Tea.

Her salt and pepper hair
falls below her waist,
and she sports cateye Ray-Bans

with a matching lime-green bikini.
She paints her toenails bright fuchsia
and etches a perfect em dash

in the middle of each nail.
No one knows
about her lookout hideaway.

If asked, she always blames
her farmer's tan on gardening
without a proper sunhat or work gloves.

She listens to Adele on her iPod
and knows all the words to "Hello" by heart.
When her father takes his long afternoon naps

and her sister weeds the garden
or carries a stepladder into the apple orchard
with a pair of sleepy cats trailing behind her,

Emily unlocks the chest
filled with forty hand-sewn booklets
and reads one poem aloud

until it's burned to memory's dark chamber.
Then she rips the page from its red yarn binding,
cuts it into confetti, and tosses it to the wind.

Silent flurries of letting go,
secret furies of a life unlived.

Chimera

The current stretches
like silvered amnion,
rock flexes

its translucence.

Light furs
an ashen wake
in the forever sound

of water.

From shallow depths,
a mythic beast
swells this rapid caul.

It is her time.

Beneath the moon

a gypsy moth
lights upon
barbed wire.

Laura unlocks Emily Dickinson's aging dreams. She awakens our mythic selves and pulls back the veil. With fearless, sharp eyes she sees beauty and shares it with us. Come bask in her poems.

— CHERYL DENISE, Author of *What's in the Blood*

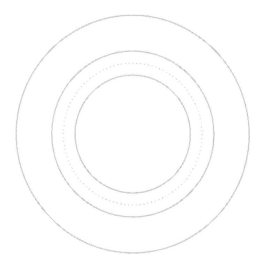

6 Flash Essays from *A Ten Minute Walk*

ESTHER MASCHIO

||||||||||||||||||||||||||||||||||||||||||||||||||||||||||||

An Introduction

After a quarter century of being a commercial artist, wife and mother, I had a transformative opportunity to study etching in Italy. My love for graphics and finding a studio dedicated to this process in a tiny mountain village in Tuscany was a dream come true.

Since 2003, for six weeks every fall, I have been in residency learning more and more about the etching process. It has become a second home and in addition to creating art, I began to write about the people there and the friendships made in a place I dare to call euphoric.

Silent Company

Every summer I cannot wait to once again experience the heights and depths of an intensive form of printmaking: etching. Among my blessings, I count a month's time and a place to work uninterrupted to create art. Within an outstanding, almost euphoric setting of a tiny Tuscan village called Valdottavo, nestled in the low Aipi Apuane Mountains, lies an old stone barn turned into a studio which awaits anyone willing or crazy enough to take on the challenges of the labor of etching.

Delays at Logan Airport in Boston give me time to contemplate wonderment. I think of such things as being able to fly through the air, cross oceans in a matter of hours, and descend into a land thousands of miles away. I think of man's beginnings and how long it took us to arrive at this time and place, first by walking upright, digging soil, using fire, figuring out which earth could be fashioned into art, tools, weapons, and eventually airplanes. Then I think how much time it takes to make a painting or a sculpture or write a book. In the context of evolutions, discoveries, and inventions, creating art seems to take no time at all. I try to keep in mind that my brief stay making art at Studio Camnitzer is also a step in the continuum of mankind.

It is daunting for me to think how many others before me have developed the materials necessary to use in creating art on brass: emulsions, resists, solvents, corrosives, cleaners, oils, cutters, grinders, multiple hand tools, exposure lights, computers, acetates, inks, papers, and the etching press itself. All these items and more had to be created, put into a vortex and funneled here to the Studio in order for me to create a work of art.

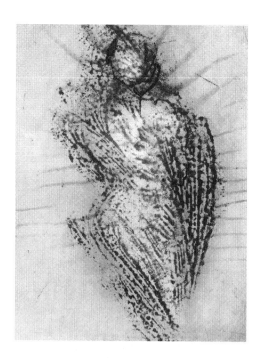

The Little Ad

A ½" ad given to me years ago began my studies in etching and the start of my relationship with Italy and its people. The tiny ad became my contact with Luis Camnitzer, who owns property in Valdottavo, a small rural town eight miles north of Lucca in Western Tuscany. This property consists of his private residence and an old stone barn converted into Studio Camnitzer. A short distance up the hill is another stone building, an upgraded farmhouse, Le Vigne, used as a residence for visiting artists. The Studio opened in 1975.

My first year at the Studio in 2003 held many beginnings: a return to etching and etching with multiple plates, residing in a foreign country, speaking—or attempting to speak—another language. No one in the village speaks English. No need to. Stranieri are rare.

The brochure said the distance between the studio and LeVigne was a ten minute walk. It made no mention that it was a mountain hike, steep and winding. The "ten minute walk" was a good thirty minutes. The hills were the Aipi Apuane Mountains, also known as the Lower Alps. After muscle aches subsided, I began to appreciate the beauty. There was a serenity here and it gave me comfort the way a warm blanket takes the chill from your bones. I was beginning to feel the renewal of my creative spirit.

The Teacher

An integral part of my creative journey in Italy is Michael, my teacher. Each year his offer to pick me up at the airport feels like the beginning of our work. At the Pisa Airport, Michael stands apart from a small crowd of people waiting to greet the passengers. Easy for me to spot, Michael always wears a black shirt and dungarees. Untanned, fair skin and of medium height, he can easily go unnoticed, which I have come to understand is his preference.

In 1985, Michael came here to study etching at age 28 and did so for two consecutive summers before returning to his native Germany. After those two years, he was hired to teach what he had learned so well, and he has been doing so at the Studio ever since.

As a teacher, Michael is patient, unassuming, unimposing and surely possesses another sense over the five with which we are endowed. He can tell by the sound of a grinder or the can of spray paint whether you are on track. He knows without the timer, although he uses one, how long to expose or etch metal. He lifts his thinly shaped glasses to his forehead to examine an etching detail, and without hesitation he intuits the length of time it will take for a solution to dry on a plate depending on the time of day.

Each year, the morning after my arrival, Michael will wait for me at the Studio by the large open shed. My fourth year in 2006 was no different. That year offered a perfect, warm sunny morning to start the journey. Michael and I climbed the familiar outside stairs to the second floor of the Studio, which houses the computers and etching presses. The boards on three of the wooden steps were still loose and they made a familiar welcoming sound, summoning me to work. Two presses stood silently in the center of the room. Sentries of it all, they patiently waited for the multitude of steps to be taken before paper and plate could be laid on them and a print made. I pulled up my favorite padded leather stool next to the computer where Michael sat waiting for the image I had chosen for this year's work. Indeed, it was a fine day to begin the creative process.

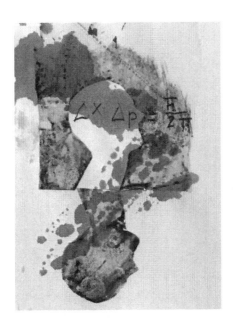

||||||||||||||||||||||||||||||||||||||||||||||||||||||||||||||||||||||||||||||||||||||||

Il Muro

Before my third year working at the Studio in 2005, I spent several days being a tourist in Florence. On one quiet side street, man and nature together had created a palimpsest of form and color on a wall, each pushing and pulling against the other. The wall was perhaps 10' wide and 20' high. A figure filled the space. The surface was layer upon layer of peeling paint which, in its own natural deterioration, took on the shape of the head and shoulders of a giantess.

Almost airless, the damp of the night lingered here well into the morning. Little sun entered due to the narrow street and the height of the buildings. Large grey stones cobbled the street and slender sidewalks. Over hundreds of years, traffic from carriages to cars to pedestrians have worn smooth furrows in the granite pavement. Only a short distance away stands the Uffizi Gallery with tourists avidly taking in a little bit of history.

Here, there were no museum guards or pedestals roping off treasured paintings. Flash cameras and touching were allowed and passersby must have thought this straniera a bit odd spending so much time by this old wall. I did almost everything short of kneeling in prayer. I was transfixed by this masterpiece perhaps seen only by me in this public space. I trembled and fumbled for the camera lest this image disappear before I could record it. I stayed until my body and mind quieted.

The wall figure in Florence was the Protectoress of all the women that I have created in my art since early adulthood. The figure came to me as an apparition, suddenly and without expectation. Seeing her was a call to me to pull up all that my mind, body, and soul had taken in these many years, to look back in order to move forward.

This did not wash over me as I was photographing the Wall, but something told me it was an important moment and image. She, on the Wall, was larger than life, as is spirit.

Rosa

Typically, I don't work from photos, but packing Rosa's photo in with my art for Studio work made sense in 2006. This candid shot of a friend, of a woman who was an integral part of the fabric in the little hill town of Valdottavo, wasn't just a photo of a dear friend. Rosa had become an icon, and she represented for me all the women in Valdottavo in their complexities and diversities.

I met Rosa in 2003, the first year I worked at the Studio. For years she cooked and brought meals to the Studio for the visiting artists. She also tended the surrounding gardens. The day that I met her, she was dressed in a simple sleeveless blouse and skirt and hefting a large watering can. It was early, but the heat was rising, and she wanted to finish her gardening chores before midmorning.

During that first meeting, I nervously tried the modicum of Italian I had been learning in a continuing education course at home. I introduced myself to Rosa. Her answer was enthusiastic, and it came with more Italian than I could grasp, but her body language said it all: I was welcomed.

In 2006, as I prepared to make a preliminary drawing of Rosa for the etching, I looked at her photo and realized that I knew only bits and pieces of her life. Rosa came to Valdottavo with her family from Sicily at age eleven, and later she married a widowed man who spent many hours at the local bar after his work while Rosa raised seven children in a tiny apartment. Somehow my leap of faith was needed in order to show her complexities that stretched from her endurance to her loving nature.

The challenges this project presented ran in every direction. There was the depth of Michael's friendship with Rosa. Over the years, I had observed their tender, close relationship. Still, Michael stayed true to his teacherly ways. When I said that I wanted to create an etching of Rosa, he simply asked: "What do you need for the drawing?" Long days into nights followed as I created the drawing, then the etching where Michael's eyes as master printer served as my guide.

At the end of my Studio stay, Rosa invited Michael and me to dinner. Minutes away from the Studio, Rosa lives in a third floor apartment that consists of two tiny rooms: a living-dining room and a bedroom. The kitchen is tucked in the hallway between the two rooms.

That evening, Michael and I sat in Rosa's living-dining room and enjoyed a meal that arrived in courses: spaghetti in a simple basil and tomato sauce; sage and garlic roasted chicken; sautéed squash blossoms stuffed with meat cheese and bread, flavored with nutmeg; formaggio; wine; Sicilian almonds cooked in hard candy syrup served with espresso. Good simple food. Expecting the best of ingredients is an Italian national attitude.

At the end of our meal, it was time for me to give Rosa the etching that I made from the photo of her. In my best Italian, I said, "For you, for your friendship, cara Rosa, in gratitude for all you have given me all these years." Rosa trembled as I gave her the package. Her surprise was complete when she saw the gift was an etching of her. She embraced it to her bosom as she has done with photos of family, and she said to Michael: "Now they will know I was here."

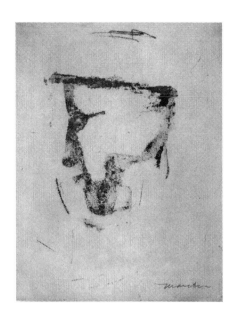

Women of the Hills

During my trip to Florence in 2005, I visited the Badia Fiorentina, a monastery and convent near the Bargello Museum. I sat at the back of the church by the main door where, upon entering, one clearly crosses into another world. From a bright, noisy, entangled city, the change is like entering a cave—one hallowed and bejeweled.

When the nuns emerged from the altar's side door, they moved with a certain grace across the holy platform. The white robes enveloped them and seemed to move independently of their occupants. In their devotion, they are closed off from worldly distractions. The nuns live on a spiritual plane, using repetitions of prayer and other rituals to stay focused.

I wondered in my own silence if these praying women were any different from the Women of the Hills, the ones that I have become so familiar with and fond of. We are all cloistered by rituals regardless of our lifestyles. Are the Women of the Hills any less holy caring for their loved ones than these invisible women kneeling in prayer? Is there a real difference between cooking and praying? Though different in genre, both are done daily and both meet needs through ritual.

During my years working at the Studio, I observed closely the women of Valdottavo. Their daily routines of walking to the grocery store, cleaning, or gardening were to me holy rituals, the equal of praying nuns. With these daily and diverse observations, my path became clear. It was connection to women, my subject matter, and this place in the hills. All this brought me a certain joy and a feeling of settling in. There came a happy anticipation for the unexpected, and how I, the interpreter, could spin these insights around to tell a visual story. I do all of this with a silent nod to the women artists who, in past centuries, went without recognition. And now, in this time and place, I summon them, and they stand with me when I am immersed in my work.

Women who make their mark do so in ways direct and indirect. Etching, such a precise art, to bring forth shapes, shadows, images that show and don't show, that are present in their vanishing, that suggest and evoke rather than tell. Straightforward, confident clear writing that orients us in time and space, the here and now and then and there, takes us on Esther's journey with her, seeing as she sees, wondering, wandering, taking it all in, the women of the hills, Michael, Rosa, the wonder of such a place and the artist who goes there for renewal until we are all the protecting angel on the wall.

— **EBERLY BARNES**, Writer, Teacher, and Happy Wanderer

Following Adventure

JEANETTE LUISE EBERHARDY

Once I entered a season of doubt. First I became ill and new tools
were needed to heal. Thus began my adventure. Along the way, I
encountered dangerous winds and a dark walk. Strangers appeared
with clues for my next steps. I learned that exploring my story matters.
And crossing the threshold between my inner and outer worlds, I was
guided by a wisdom far greater than anything I had ever experienced.

In my forties, my days were filled with a family life that I cherished. My
two daughters were thriving at ages fifteen and ten. My work as a business
developer in the senior living industry helped to support my family. My
husband seemed to be engaged in his accomplishments. We had a home
in a small coastal town south of Boston, and we enjoyed sharing time
with friends in our community. My passion for gardening, for the earth,
grew during those years. The care that I learned to give plants echoed
the attention that I was giving my family. Nothing mattered more than
creating my family after a childhood without a secure home. Yet, I felt this
nudge inside me: my work was not enough. What could that mean?

With the unrelenting pace of family life, I pushed aside this quiet
nudge of unease. However, my body began to speak for itself and demand
my attention—unexpected fainting spells, unexplained numbness in
my limbs, fibrous growths in the wall of my uterus, and more. When
results from every exotic medical test revealed no problems, my doctors
focused on hormonal changes. A team of specialists decided this was an
expression of migraine symptoms without the actual headache. They said
this can happen to some women. They recommended a plan increasingly
dependent on intense drugs as the symptoms worsened. I went along with

their recommendations until one day, at the library, I learned that one of the side effects of the latest prescription was addiction, and there was no known way to stop taking that drug.

Feeling disoriented and never knowing when the symptoms would return, I was unable to trust the answers provided. The only thought I had was this: I needed to find someone with tools other than a prescription pad.

My search began with a gift from my family. They knew something was wrong, and they wanted to help. They surprised me with a health retreat in Western Massachusetts. Their gift became my first experience where "strange little helpmates" began to appear. Myths told throughout the centuries show others—often strangers—providing useful clues at the very moment that a person needs guidance. During that retreat, I was introduced to acupuncture. Symptoms that I struggled with for years began to change after one acupuncture treatment at the retreat center. I didn't know it then, but this experience helped me to open to new perspectives on healing.

New ideas and "strange little helpmates" are fine, but I had absorbed Western society's beliefs, such as taking a pill to fix yourself. Healing processes? I had rarely encountered illness—even colds—except for now. Still, I knew it was time to listen to the language of my body, to make the effort to hear and to heed the warnings. I was released into the humility of my own ignorance on how to maintain my well-being.

After three months working with a new acupuncturist back home, the unexpected, unexplained symptoms began to vanish. During this same time, I read widely on acupuncture and on other practices shared by healers from Eastern traditions. Curiosity was reawakened in me. Based on a recommendation from my acupuncturist, I attended a one-day seminar on meditation techniques. Some of these techniques were simple enough that in one day I integrated them into my daily practices. I also began to listen to beautiful chants. My heart opened to the sounds of this music. Such simple practices—especially the breathing techniques—became the tools that I needed to pay closer attention to my inner self.

In my family line, knowledge on true healing did exist. I remember my grandmother kept two books at her bedside, a bible and a guide to herbs for healing, both in her native language, German. *Das Buch der Krauter* showed the uses for herbs, both aromatic and essential plants. During visits with her when I was in college, I didn't appreciate the importance of her deeper understanding of healing processes. She understood some things about replenishing the nutrients in the soil of the soul for new life to flourish. It took me decades to rediscover her wisdom for myself. As I look back, writer Patricia Hampl's thoughts on memory begin to make sense to me. During those new experiences with acupuncture and meditation, "I wasn't 'trying to remember' something. More like this: I was being remembered. Being remembered into a memory ... "

After one year, I returned to my general practitioner to measure the status of the fibrous growths. The scan of my body showed no evidence of any growths. "How did you do this?" my doctor asked. I told her about the work with acupuncture, meditation, and breathing exercises. "Yes," she acknowledged, "My female patients report that these interventions can be helpful."

My response was quick: "You owe it to your female clients to tell them about these options."

How is it possible for a woman to create a home filled with love and care for her daughters and for her husband, but not feel she belonged there herself? I was largely unaware of the stranger that I had become to myself until healing processes were reawakened in me. Meditation became my teacher. Dreams returned. While my older daughter attended college, I began an MFA program in writing, the degree I really wanted when I pursued graduate school the first time.

As I explored my inner world, the feeling of joy began to visit me. My spirit harmonized, and I imagined new possibilities for my work as a teacher and writer. Then the wind changed. A certain darkness followed.

A deep fault line in my relationship with my husband revealed itself. At that moment, I was preparing to enter my last year in a graduate writing program, and my younger daughter was preparing for college. You would have recognized me in my writing classes. I was the one wearing a grin from ear-to-ear, unable to contain my happiness for this new learning. I felt that these studies would lead me to the work I was meant to pursue. Still, the cracks in the surface of my marriage couldn't be ignored. After nearly twenty-five years of creating a loving family, I knew that I had to give up one of my most cherished values: honoring one's family by keeping it together—at all costs.

If these destructive winds needed to blow through my life, let it be, I thought, though I had no idea what that would bring. Already I was reading far outside my constructed reality. In meditation I experienced the shattering of an invisible shield that surrounded me. By this time, the powers of my concentration were strong enough to observe the shards of my marriage scattered everywhere.

To my acupuncturist I said, "Keep me standing." No, that's not true. I didn't say that right away. First, I hid my face in my hands. There were no words for the power of sadness that filled my body. I had entered the land of grieving, and I had no idea how to move through the territory.

With the help of an experienced team of healers, I learned to trust the hard work of grieving and the wisdom of my body. Each healer helped in their own way to keep me from shutting down while dreams and metaphysical inner experiences combined to show a more transparent self. My therapist listened to my dreams. My cranial osteopath asked where the hurt or the memory of hurt presented itself in my body. And when my acupuncturist asked how I was doing, he listened for the answer before I spoke my first word. Together these experiences revealed vital connections among mind, body, emotions, and spirit. This may sound complicated, but my goal was quite simple. I didn't want to be the person one meets at a party with anger bottled up inside her.

When I allowed myself to feel the sadness of letting go, my heart opened wider. Alone in the evenings, I cried. Then in meditation the next morning, I felt my heart open as I walked back and forth across the intersection of loss and love. This was not a single event, it happened over and over. So much so that I began to understand there was a deep relationship between suffering and the expanding capacity for kindness. Still, the walk through that dark night felt long. No matter how much I wished for short cuts, there were none for me. The walk was long.

As I continued this journey, I saw the adventure in others' stories. I began to appreciate that we are all participating in myths that are waiting to be realized. Older women showed me enduring qualities that carried them through hardships. At a time when a master printmaker could not draw, she described to me how she imagined drawing pictures in clouds on her commute to a commercial art job. She showed me the strong image of who she was and how she stayed connected to herself through hardships.

Another woman provided a powerful warning to keep going on my journey. In her eighth decade, she returned to letters she wrote in the 1940s when she worked on world hunger relief efforts. In those letters, she described her adventures flying on cargo planes to India before civilians were allowed to do so. Then, in her 80s, she realized the power in those stories and wanted to transform them into art. Once, when I gave her a ride to our local writers' group, she told me how her husband left her for a woman much younger than he when she was in her 70s. She felt that she had wasted her emotions for a decade on that experience. During that ride to our writing group, her message was clear: "Don't waste it. Don't waste your creative energy. I wasted mine, and now it is too late to write the stories that I need to tell." Today I keep her photo in an open pantry between my kitchen and my study, so I must pass it every day and remember her instructions: Don't waste your life.

My divorce came after I gave up my consulting practice and returned to graduate school for writing. Then the global economic meltdown happened in 2008. There was no turning back to my former consulting work. During this time, I heard the president of Barnard College on a book tour say there was a disturbing rising statistic: middle–aged divorced women with degrees were becoming the new poor. I sat in the audience and thought, Yes, I am becoming one of them.

Keep me standing. There was an edge of pleading in this request to my acupuncturist each time that I met with him. Help me manage my stress so I don't become ill again. The way was becoming clearer, I knew my true work was teaching and writing. Did I have enough in savings to survive until I found a way to support myself while performing this particular work?

In the act of continuing to stand and to heal, I was able to sustain the power to respond in my own way to the global economic crisis. The antidote to the terror that I felt during the meltdown was to find individuals who were trying to help the next generation think about their work in purposeful ways. If the entire financial system was full of fakery, who was trying to think in a different way? Transformations based on my new writing skills began to unfold as I interviewed global social entrepreneurs. One opportunity led to another, starting with a friend introducing me to another friend. I met a woman originally from India who built youth employment networks in 55 countries, another woman from Norway who built an international women's network to encourage female leadership in business, and a Brazilian social entrepreneur who designed digital creative communities to engage youth in dialogues about meaningful work. Each had been through their own personal crisis and an adventure that changed their work in positive ways. While I had not ventured outside the U.S., global travel to forums designed by these social entrepreneurs followed. I gave workshops on creativity, writing, and storytelling in Egypt, Sweden, Italy, Germany, and the Czech Republic. During this give-and-take time, I shared my newfound knowledge and received the wisdom of their adventures. Each experience proved to be a point of departure into the unknown. I was learning how to work beyond myself.

During this same time of grieving and growing, I felt compelled to carry on the tradition of storytelling with my daughters. I made artists' books gathering together images of my grandmother, my mother, and my daughters. While I grieved my losses, it was my instinct to engage in re-remembering across generations.

This adventure transformed my relationship with my daughters. It deepened intimate connections with myself and with them. I showed myself how not to fear an important adventure. I showed my daughters perseverance and the active engagement in the evolution of true self. Now they are showing their children, my grandchildren, how to maintain a healthy balance between inner and outer experiences by learning to pay attention to their own questions on the purpose of their lives.

Eventually I found my work as a teacher of writing at an art college. Today I encourage student artists to write in their expressive, unpretentious, authentic voices. I share mindful practices with them to encourage compassion toward self and others so they may feel courage on their own adventures and in that act, respect their own stories. Repetition of this daily work is essential. It has its own momentum, leading to surprising moments of more and more transformations. Now I share what I have learned myself: Your story matters.

||

We women need to be our own biggest advocates, and I appreciate Eberhardy's "take charge" manifesto. Is there any possible physical or mental complaint that a doctor can't blame on women at middle-age? Take it from Jeanette and don't wait until you're a stranger in your own home and family to find the support you need.

— CHRISTINE ARVIDSON, Editor of *The Love of Baseball: Essays by Lifelong Fans*

From Whence Cometh My Help: How Black Girl Magic Can Change Appalachia

SHEILA COLEMAN-CASTELLS

My life began in earnest when I moved to West Virginia twelve years ago. I know that sounds strange, given that I was at that time forty-four years old, a mature woman, a divorced single mother of an eight-year-old son, and a seasoned professional. And yet, moving to this mountain in Preston County, West Virginia, felt to me like a re-birth and a homecoming, all at the same time. I found that the social and cultural mores of dedication to family, reverence for hard work, and loyalty to community values were right at home with how I had been raised in urban Washington, D.C. by Southern parents who came from small African-American communities in Virginia and North Carolina. Even though I came here not knowing anyone, nor having a job here (I owned a very small consulting business and had a clientele throughout the U.S.), I knew that relocating to the snowy, windy mountaintop, THIS was what I had to do, and that it was an important time in the history of the state of West Virginia and indeed all of Appalachia. And I knew that this was my place, my time, and that I was finally "home."

I cannot say that it has always been easy to be here in the Mountain State, but I can say that never in my life have I felt like my skills and talents have been used in such an important way as they are here in West Virginia. Contrary to what many have said to me, and how many people believe, being an African American woman in Appalachia is not a deficit in any way; if anything, it is an astounding asset, gold in the pocket regarding understanding how and why we are in the social situation in which we find ourselves here, and so too the insight as to how to break out of the prison of expectations, stigmas, and inertia that can (but doesn't have to) define our lives.

I deeply understand this because being a Black woman in this culture is to live trapped in a sort of amber, except that it is neither beautiful nor valuable, but it is just as confining. Many people assume that they know what your life is like, and that it is defined by cultural disenfranchisement, stagnation, and blockage by the "powers that be." It would be correct to say that for many Black Appalachians, called "Affrilachian" by the poet Frank X Walker, the feeling and the reality of being socially entrapped in poverty and lack of access in these hills is very real. The hurdles that most White Appalachians have to climb to escape this miasma of lack, while steep, does pale in comparison to what the Affrilachian has to endure, especially if she is female. After all, in less than a generation, any white Appalachian can shed their culture and take on another in the urban centers of our country, looking back from the foliage-covered balconies of the Ivy League to recount an elegy of their hillbilly days. But the Affrilachian woman cannot shed her Blackness, as the mountains cannot become the shore. So it is true that these barriers are tangible and while the Appalachian culture can often be strict and unyielding in its need to confine the intellectual and spiritual gifts of people of color, Black women who wish to emerge from the imposed confines of race and class and redefine themselves and their talents in the larger world are compelled to use their many gifts to change straw into gold where they find themselves, in these storied hills of green.

It is often said that "fortune favors the bold," and in these times of great cultural shift in Appalachia, there is a critical need for a renewed spirit of innovation and investment in all of our people here. The old guards, those who have controlled the region for at least the last one hundred and seventy-five years, have run out of economic ideas for how we plan our future. Sadly, they have only ever had one real idea: The concept of extractive energy and the industrialized form of slavery that was set up to fuel the economic engine of the state. This engine drove over the bodies of most of the working folks here, and now we see ourselves left behind while the rest of the country moves forward.

While coal is currently sputtering to a halt, now the same powers that be bestow upon us the promise of natural gas, touted as the panacea to our economic woes, using a furtive and poisonous extractive technology that will tear up the earth beneath our feet, foul our water, and leave the land with less value and our residents poor and in ill-health, yet again. This movie has been seen before, and it didn't end well, but our leaders in Appalachia are hell-bent on looping it again and again, and convincing us that it is literally the only show in town and that we have no choice but to make it our story. This is the crux of the lie, that we in Appalachia are stuck watching and indeed living out this played-out movie. Alas, we are not actually captive to this show, we are only taught to THINK that we are. We are ripe for new ideas, and we are rich with burgeoning industry that stems from our own abilities to adapt and change to changing times. As Black women, or indeed ANY Appalachian women, we have a huge advantage in a hide-bound patriarchal culture that suffers from a terminal lack of new inspiration, because we are forced every day to change and innovate in order to survive and ensure the success of our children. We have the experience of doing what we do: Making do using improvisation, innovation, and invention to change things for the better. The only thing stopping us is US. The only thing we don't have is our own voice, spoken to power, that demands better investment in our own people and their own innovation to solve their own problems.

Why do I say that WE are the barrier to our own success? It is because we women, especially women of color, often accept the miniscule space created for us by this culture, and we pay far more rent for it than is merited. I have often gotten stares and sometimes, even jeers, the cold shoulder and outright sabotage from white men in power in this state, from the low to the high. However, I have a strategic advantage. I am smart, I am resilient, and I will never, ever be told "NO." "You can't" simply doesn't compute. The answer is never really "no." Perhaps it is not now, not here, or not with you, but never, ever is it NO if indeed it is to be so.

My sister-models of perseverance in this struggle for the soul of my state have shown me that they have plowed through massive boulders under the soil to break the ground free and plant nourishing food for thought on steep slopes. They have blasted through rock to create tunnels to keep from climbing on horseback over the snow-laden mountains, and they have navigated treacherous rivers under threat of death to get where they wanted to go, portering the goods that they needed for their communities. In short, the disapproval and resistance to new and enlightening ideas is but a mere annoyance in the face of the crushing need for a better way to uplift my neighbors, my people.

It is my right and my responsibility to bring this life-giving water of understanding and new ideas to my community, to lift the boats of all my neighbors, regardless of their backgrounds, for we have no choice in this matter: it is a life or death struggle. Either we, as women and especially women of color, save Appalachia one family, one school, one church, one town at a time, or we will all die together under the scourge of worthless, 19th century ideas, back-breaking work that results in early death and disability, and the loss of the TRUE soul of our state: our people and their innate and relentless ingenuity.

Currently, heroin and methamphetamine addiction are the evidence that we are not at all reaching those who need new ideas and a renewed sense of purpose. Rampant drug and alcohol addiction is an outward sign of our own failure to show our children and neighbors that hope for a better life free of physical and psycho-social pain is real, and that this hope, these solutions can be actualized in the present day. We are all guilty of a failure to preach the gospel of a new day and a new way to our neighbors, and to actualize it by providing the bread of empowerment and dignity to people. Doing this would mean that the false lure of a cheap high is not attractive, because real life is FAR better than smack. I know what this is like. Growing up in 1960s-70s Washington D.C., I saw the effects of a social and economic change that rendered people redundant, hopeless, and unmoored, and it literally took 30 years or more to reclaim the soul of a city from the clutches of drug abuse. Sadly, however, once that happened, countless lives had been dashed upon the rocks, never to be recovered. Unlike today, when people are beginning to have empathy for those who are struggling with addiction, then our citizens of color were treated like pariahs, no better than mangy feral dogs in the street left to be consumed by the plague of crime and sickness, until they died in abandoned houses and in gutters. Their lives meant nothing not just because they were poor junkies, with no social value.

They were also Black in the capital of the free world, staining the white marble monuments to greater men whose lives were perceived to actually mean something in the larger narrative of our country than those who died ignominiously at the feet of the Founding Fathers. The Black crackhead, who might have been a father or a mother, a former U.S. government worker, a homeowner, a Vietnam Veteran who never got his or her due, why they were simply collateral damage to an economic and cultural shift that saw us investing in knowledge workers whose minds were far more important than those whose labor was invested in their hands or their backs.

The Black woman in history has long held her daughters and sons while they died as cannon fodder in this culture war, young men who have a one-in-three chance of making it to age 35, only to be incarcerated on petty charges. She has raised her daughter's babies while their Mother chased a paycheck in a far-away city, or ran after a man who she hoped would give her a stable life with the proverbial picket fence and the two-car garage which hardly ever comes. She has nursed her own man through his struggles as he has fought with the cultural demons. She has held two jobs, paid the bills, sent her children to college, worked in her church, taken in her sister's children, enrolled in community college and gotten her GED, then her Bachelor's or her

Master's degree, only to be denied a raise in her job while younger White men and women have sped past her. She has remained alone and kept to herself, knowing that she had only her God to maintain her and her sanity, relying on that God to sustain her through lean times and to keep her loved ones safe. She keeps her sidewalk clean and buys plants to put in window boxes, so she knows how to plant seeds and maintain them while watching them grow. She is the soul of Appalachia, and she can make a huge difference to our economic and social trajectory if she is released from the stifling amber of cultural entrapment that is racism and classism.

Were it in my power, I would take a sledgehammer to the amber, breaking her free from this de facto prison that stifles her ideas under the unspoken thought that "you're not valuable." But to do that might be to destroy her and the very precious value that she offers the world, for you cannot crush the amber without destroying the beauty of the figure trapped there. So, I take a different and more wide-ranging approach: I want to get to her before she is trapped in that golden prison. I have to show her, while young, that she has no need to adhere to outmoded cultural ways of being that require her to get "permission" from anyone to be her authentic self. No one who ever asked permission from others would be allowed to let their talents roam free. I say to her that she must take her liberties and adopt a "can do" spirit, not waiting for anyone or anything to give her permission to create and innovate. She needs to speak her truth, from her youth, and allow her voice to be heard in this land, in these hills. I know that the young Black woman is one of many champions of Appalachia, and she must start in her own space, her own block, or her own town, with the men in power, and force them to listen to her voice. She needs to charm, wheedle, manipulate, cajole, pressure, undermine, or blast her way out, and eventually topple the structures that keep all of us from trying new ideas and new measures to change our lives. No tool in her toolbox must go unused. She must know that this is the only way to sweep out the old, putrefied ways and that we cannot and should not tiptoe around the need, in fact the duty, to do this right now.

If the old ways had worked, her mother and grandmother would not be where they are right now, with the two jobs, the lost dreams, and the endless investment in cleaning up societal messes not of her making, in silence. It is time for the Affrilachian, the woman of color of Appalachia, and indeed ALL women in our mountain home, to adopt a new and radical strategy: forward, with no retreat nor surrender. Her ideas, her perseverance, and her fortitude are the salvation of this region. Why does it fall to her? Because the Affrilachian woman has no cushion of privilege to fall back on should she fail. It is do or die for her and her children. And she has always been willing to go to the proverbial mat for that which she believes. Appalachia needs saving, but there are no "white hats" from the outside to come to the rescue. The solution to our problems lies within, and lies with our own people. The Affrilachian woman is the stone that the builders rejected that cornerstone of strength, ingenuity, and resilience that can lead the way if we collectively endeavor to take the cultural baggage OUT of the way. Her voice, her ideas, her shining mind is the one that can make a better way.

A few years before I came to live in West Virginia, I dreamt of climbing a mountain during rain and harsh weather (my neighborhood was in the throes of Hurricane Isabel at the time) and I woke up with the phrase from the Christian Scriptures: "I lift up mine eyes to the hills from whence cometh my help." Little did I know that I would indeed be climbing a mountain in a strong rainstorm several years later to move into my "holy mountain," a little cottage on a ridgetop in Preston County. Over the years, I have worked in the state of West Virginia, marveling at the amazing minds and hearts that I have met along the way. I have seen that the answers to our social and economic problems are actually all around us, in the intellect and the fortitude of our own people. No group is more maligned and excluded than is my own, the African American woman. Yet with her own strength and ability to take nothing and make it into something, her own special alchemy, she is indeed the prestidigitator, the magician that we need to change our way of life.

When you change the way you look at things, the things you look at change. It is time for us to use our Black Girl magic to make these mountains our own, and change the face of Appalachia with the beauty of our own distinct intellect. If Appalachia is wise, it will allow her to wave her wand and help create a new culture, suitable for us all, in these beautiful green hills.

Don't fashion me into a maiden
that needs saving from a dragon.
I am the dragon,
and I will eat you whole.
— Unknown

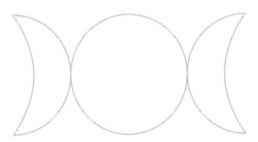

Slasher—Story of a Teenager

ANGELA GIRON

It's December 31st, 1966. From a palette of Yardley eye shadows, I dip a tapered brush and apply a soft pink shade under the arch of my brows. Maybe I'll paint a purple flower on my cheekbone. My older sister Josie and I share a bedroom again. We have ever since our move from the Golden Gate barrio to Cypress Street. This house was expensive for my folks, but it only has three bedrooms rather than four. We forfeited a bedroom, unpaved spaces for paved sidewalks with palm trees. We traded Spanish accents for nondescript American English sounds. Bitchin', far out. We've stepped up.

My parents have one bedroom, my little brother Georgie has the tiny bedroom down the middle hall; and my sister Josie and I share the master bedroom with two closets. My eldest brother Ramon's been in the Air Force for about a year, I think. I forget. I haven't seen him in some time. He didn't even come home for Christmas as he only had a couple of days' leave, and besides, he has a girl who lives near the base in Victorville, so he spent Christmas with her and her family.

Last time I saw Ramon was when I was in the psyche Zoo. He came to visit me one afternoon and by the time he left he was scared of me. It was great to inflict fear in him for a change. I must have really seemed crazy, jabbering away unintelligibly just so I would not have to talk to him. I discovered that there's power in madness. He broke down and cried. Right in front of me. "I'm sorry. I'm sorry, Nita. I'm sorry I went away and didn't see you through with it." See me through with what? I'd like to know. Just what the fuck did he think he could see me through with?

Wait a minute. That's not the last time I saw Ramon. Fuckin' schlock, shock treatments. They've messed up my memory. That keeps on happening. I think I'm remembering something and then it all gets screwed up in terms of place or date. I hate when that happens. Fucked up world that will take a sixteen-year-old girl's mind and mess with it like that. When my brother Eddie got back from Nam and found out what they'd done to me, boy, was he ever pissed. Eddie knows all about mind fucking.

Anyway, the last time I saw Ramon was in California last summer. I'd gone to visit Eddie. Eddie won a scholarship to an art school in Hollywood. Last summer, things were pretty difficult with my parents and even my shrink, Dr. Bernardo, thought it would be a good idea if I went and stayed with Eddie for a bit. I didn't think they'd ever let me go because I had been a runaway in L.A. earlier. I even spent a couple of weeks in the L.A. County Detention Home. So, when I was visiting Eddie, Ramon came up one weekend to see us. Eddie, his friends and I were all having a blast! We were having a party with lots of students from Eddie's art school. Then one girl, Trish, who had dropped acid, started using Eddie's paints. She began doing all these beautiful psychedelic paintings on the exterior wall near where we were barbecuing. It was pretty obvious she was tripping, but she wasn't harming anyone. Ramon got uppity and started snarling at Eddie, "What kind of shit are you exposing Anita to?" He said how he was being a bad influence on me. This bothered Eddie and caused him to rethink his lax 'tude with me. Ramon, on the other hand, then decided to take Trish home, "Get her out of the party as she was crashing from the acid." Of course, he didn't get back 'til the next morning; I know he scored with her. Sure, he fucked her. He fucks everyone. Plus, chicks like Ramon. He's dark and broody looking.

Next day Ramon wants some kind of heart-to-heart. "Hey, I mean, I know what you're going through ... Man! I spent some time in juvie, in reformatory. I know the score."

I didn't care that he did. He had his story. I had my story. It's not the same.

He tried to placate me through guilt. "It's been rough for Ma and Dad. First me, and all the bullshit I put them through, then Eddie in Nam. Now you too. You got to think about them..."

Oh yeah? Did you think about them? I have felt badly about what Mama and Daddy have had to go through but what I'm going through seems far worse.

"You see, you can learn from my mistakes." Oh really? "There's no need for you to suffer what I've suffered, regret what I've regretted." He can be such an egoist.

"...and I know you're doing better," pep talk here. "Ma says you're writing some really... interesting poetry. That's good, Anita. Put it on paper. Get the rage out and put it on paper!" He began to sound like an Evangelist.

So that was the last time I saw Ramon. Eddie's back now. He decided to move back to Phoenix and go to ASU as an art major. He's found a little apartment not too far from us and comes home for supper often. My sister Josie's also at ASU. Dad tells everyone Josie's going to be a teacher. Dad used to be a teacher an eon ago, before he married Ma, during the Depression when the educational qualifications were lower. I guess now he plans to have Josie fulfill his evaporated dream. I don't think Josie will do it. She hates ASU. It's huge and intimidating for her. Josie seems to be shrinking, becoming more invisible as the years go by. I hardly notice her presence anymore. Clearly she hates me now, she has for some time. Maybe she always has, and I never noticed it. But I'm immune to her hatred. Once I had so much attention in my family because I was so cute and smart. Now I have so much attention because I'm such a smart badass.

Josie doesn't like how I dress, wear my hair, or wear my make-up. The last couple of years I've had my hair dyed red. Sparkling Sherry, by Miss Clairol. Recently, I've dyed it dark brown with gold-streaked highlights and frizzed out curls. I think I look quite Mod, and with the crushed velvet Victorian jacket that I bought at *The Curiosity Shop* in Scottsdale over a red miniskirt and thigh high black suede boots that I'm wearing for the Canned Heat New Year's Eve concert tonight? Super Mod!

Dad wants me home by midnight. Midnight! Curfew on New Year's Eve! It's unrealistic. He said that if I could not promise to be home by midnight, I couldn't go. Promises are cheap. I promised. "Let's Spend the Night Together" is playing on the radio. All day KRIZ has been playing the top songs of the year. It's been a great year for music. The Doors is a new group I really love. I got turned on to them when I was in the psyche Zoo.

When I got moved from that batty North Wing into a more permanent residence at the hospital, Miss Carroll, my high school counselor, brought me a huge poster of Jim Morrison to place on the wall above my bed. He looks like a dark, sexy version of Christ incarnate. Morrison knows what madness is totally about. The Beatles' "Strawberry Fields Forever" begins to play as I paint a flower on my cheek. Incredible timing. I'll just make a couple of changes and oh yeah, groovy! A strawberry on my cheek is far hipper. When I was a child, I felt like it would be Strawberry Fields Forever. Not so much anymore.

Next, "20th Century Fox" plays on the radio and as I survey my image, that's exactly what I look like. A real 20th Century FOX! I zip up my thigh-high black suede boots, and they look great, but they feel looser on my calves than last month. I'm beginning to lose too much weight. I've always been petite but I'm going to disappear if I don't watch out. It's the speed, I know it. I'm shooting too much. What is it that Jagger sings? *Under my thumb ... well, I'm totally under speed's thumb, that's for sure.*

Mama peeks in, "*Mi hijita*, you will be home at midnight?" She means to make a statement, but it comes out like a question.

"Like Cinderella," I answer with a tough sarcasm. I've offered all my arguments against the curfew to no avail. What everybody else's parents let them do, is of no consequence. I'm through with trying to reason with my parents; I'm now committed to defiance.

"Daddy just worries about all the drunks that are out on New Year's Eve."

"Daddy's worried about drunks? Boy! That's a good one. My third day in the psyche Zoo some old geezer on Ritalin tried to kill me! I told both of you that then, but you certainly weren't worried enough to get me out of there, now were you?"

"Just be home by twelve," she closes the door behind her.

I finish dressing, then take a notebook from out of a bottom drawer and plunk myself on top of my twin bed, annoyed at everything/everyone. I've had this same twin bed since I was five. Since Georgie was born and grabbed my crib. They bought this Early American Maple bedroom set in Los Angeles. I wish we had never moved back from there. I was so happy in Rose Hills. We all were. I snicker sadly now as I remember the "Who do you like the best?" games that my siblings played with me. It's almost as though that was another person who would ride flaxen haired on the tire swing hanging on the peach tree. Like a distant cousin that vaguely resembles me today. I often wonder who I would be if we had just remained in California.

Jean is late. Probably painting Twiggy lashes on her bottom eyeline. Plus, she had to pick-up Candy and Rae. Then me, then Debbie. Debbie's grounded and we have to pick her up at the Taco Bell after she's snuck out of her bedroom window at nine-thirty, about the time her alcoholic mother will probably pass out. I spoke with Debbie about an hour ago. Things look good. Her mother started early on this final day of the year, and she was already weaving by seven-thirty. These are my post-jock girlfriends. When I was a freshman, I hung out with all my Chicano friends from the Golden Gate barrio and kids I met at CYO. Then when we left the barrio and moved, I had to change schools, and there were no Chicano kids hardly at all, so sophomore year I went straight from the barrio to hanging out with other baton majorettes like myself (expert from grade school), cheerleaders, Pom-Pom girls, plus Advanced courses/curriculum in the new school, all of us dating Football players and boys from Parnassus. Parnassus kids my new friends are not. They are all Mods or Hippies. They all wish they could go to Scottsdale High where the trendier hippies go. As if in a time warp, we all found ourselves by geographical allocation, at a super Jock, shitkicker school, East High, where everyone dresses and wears their hair like it's still the 1950s. Earlier last year before the psyche Zoo when I came back from being a runaway in Los Angeles with Libby from Scottsdale, my rep was ruined. Libby. Poor Libby. Now she has a baby. Darryl didn't believe it was his, maybe it wasn't, anyway they split up. She's only sixteen. Probably we'll never be friends again.

January 1966: I turn to Libby who looks oddly relieved to be getting fingerprinted. It's been quite a journey and now it's almost over. They take us for mug shots, I look at the clock, three-thirty a.m. We've been fugitives for six weeks. How the hell did they find us? I glance at Libby again, I know. I caught her talking on the phone a couple of days ago to Darryl. She swore she didn't tell him our whereabouts, but I'm sure she did. He must have told the authorities. I mean really, did she think Darryl would go for us living with this Rock & Roll band in Hollywood? Now it all seems so stupid. I never had any intention of running away to begin with. I was just helping out Libby and this other chick Diane from Scottsdale, a friend of hers. They needed a ride to Phoenix, specifically to Grand Avenue, where they could then hitchhike out of the hellhole of the Valley of the Sun.

I went to pick up Diane and Libby at an open field near the new sub-development where Libby lives. Libby's mother Katy had started working for Motorola several years ago, and they bought a brand-new house the summer after we graduated from the barrio school. It takes a good half hour to drive out there.

Driving, I scanned the sides of Granite Reef Road, where not long before the only thing you could see was the Pima Indian Reservation in the distance. Now, there was row upon row of Townhouses, Model Homes, and strange, developing, desolate looking neighborhoods with

RV Campers, boats, parked in freshly cemented double driveways. By the time Libby and Diane and I were headed for Grand Avenue, I was two hours late for supper and simply got "caught up" in the thrill of the adventure. I didn't go home that night. We stayed with this guy Diane slept with who said we had to leave the next day. Worried that they would be looking for us in my sister Josie's '56 Chevy, we dumped it behind the Pizza Hut on Central Avenue, and Diane called my house to let them know where the car was at. Now we were on the run. No home, no clothes, no money—three stupid teenagers.

The next day we roamed around Chris-town Mall and met a guy named John. He said he had a place in Glendale we could stay at. The guy he lived with was a lot older than us, maybe twenty-seven, maybe even thirty. His name was Duane and he was a bit slow, retarded really. Duane chain smoked Pall Mall Reds, and I started smoking that day.

We didn't do much in Glendale except find ways to eat. I organized Scavenger Hunts and made Diane and Libby take off their make-up, wear pig tails and comb the neighborhood at dusk, asking for cans of Campbell's soup and Spam. We even got shampoo and tampons that way. One night we went back to the parking lot at Chris-town Mall and John lowered me into a Goodwill bin, so I could get us all clothes. I found myself a cool red Batman T-Shirt. Diane and Libby were getting comfortable in Glendale. But I wanted to go to California, their original plan. Lots of runaways went to Los Angeles or San Francisco, it would be easy and fun there. Diane hesitated, having second thoughts about being a runaway. Libby too, although I could control Libby easier. She wasn't as brave a runaway as I had expected. For me it became like a game; seeing how we could survive without having to do anything drastic. You know, without becoming prostitutes or stealing purses. One can sure get "caught up" in the moment-to-moment adventure of being a fugitive. There's something wild and free about it. Everything's fated. One right or wrong move can change the course of your life. Everything's justifiable.

Over the radio on the Teen Search runaway spotlight, our names were being called over KRIZ radio to "please contact our parents." We felt famous. Libby and Diane called their homes. They were told that they could pick up anything they wanted and were free to leave again. They were gravely missing their transistor radios and hatbox hair dryers. I knew it was a bluff.

On Saturday, Libby called her boyfriend Darryl. He promised he wouldn't give away our location, that he would pick us up so that Libby and Diane could go home and get their things. I never called my parents.

On the way to Scottsdale I talked Libby into staying with me at the parking lot of Fashion Square Mall to just wait and see what would happen to Diane once she went home to collect her shit. Darryl reluctantly dropped us off and came back a half hour later to tell us that no sooner had Diane walked into her house than two cop cars arrived and hauled her off to Juvie. I grabbed Libby's hand, so did Darryl, but he lost and so we ran off.

That Saturday was five weeks ago. And now here we are sitting in the Sheriff's office in West Hollywood, waiting to get carted off to Juvie after all.

When we first arrived in Hollywood, I changed Libby's and my name, and aged us to nineteen. Eighteen sounded too suspicious. I renamed Libby Roxanne, called her Roxie, and named myself Valerie. We even went over to the Social Security office in Hollywood and easily got Social Security cards in these names. I had what I thought was a believable story for all the new people we met. The story was that we were from Ohio and had been hitchhiking across the country for six months. We met this rock band at Griffith Park and moved in with them. Libby, or rather Roxie, got involved with the drummer.

I had always anticipated that the day might come when we'd get busted. I knew that the Los Angeles County Detention Home was close to the county hospital because my Aunt Carmen used to work there. I had an Ace in the hole. The Ace was a single edged razor, the dull side further protected by a band-aid to be hidden behind my ear. Earlier tonight when we got home, Mike, the drummer, slipped and called Roxanne, Libby. Oh well, I knew then that we were only moments away from the bust. I took the razor discreetly out of my wallet and wedged it behind my ear. Five minutes later the cops were at the house, handcuffing us and taking us to the station.

Riding in the squad car on the Hollywood Freeway to the L.A. County Detention Home, I feel completely numb. I glance at Libby, but we don't even talk. Lights flicker; Melrose, Normandie exits skirt by; I wonder where the night might lead. It's four-thirty in the morning when we get to Juvie. The Head Matron lazily takes the reports from the officers and ushers us into a waiting room. Minutes later Libby's taken away, I wait and plan the moment. I'm going to slit my wrists so that I'll be taken to the county hospital. Tomorrow I can easily run away from there.

I barely finger the blade when I'm taken to another room with showers. I'm told to disrobe. I take off my red Batman T-shirt, jeans and sandals; the floor is concrete and ice cold. A different Matron appraises me and says, "We're supposed to have you all take showers before you go on the inside—but it's so damn late and cold."

I just stare at a crack on the concrete. "Ok, honey, bend your head down." I obey. She runs her hands briskly over my head for final inspection. It's a frozen moment. There's a dull clink on the concrete. "What the hell's that!?"

I look up. "What the hell do you think it is?"

She smacks me across the face with the bloody palm of her hand, sending me flying across the room close to the shower stalls. I stare sullenly at my Ace on the floor. I learn a hard lesson about solitary confinement.

My first day back at East High, lunch time, cafeteria, I head for the Jock table as "Good Vibrations" plays on the jukebox. Having found the textural oddly-colored red and purple Lettermen sweaters clad onto popular jock students, I arrive at their table and stand to the tune of deafening silence. It feels as if the blood drains from my body when suddenly an uproarious clapping begins at another table, beckoning me. It's the incorrigible girls. They look more beautiful and hipper than I had ever remembered them. Saved by their applause, I carry my tray over to them, not once looking back.

They begin non-stop questioning.

"What was it like being a runaway?"

"Did you make it to the Whiskey A Go Go?" Candy breathed.

I found my place. For a bit.

My notebook is still annoyingly blank. Back in my bedroom I look up at my Jim Morrison poster for inspiration. There are frayed Scotch taped edges from moving the poster from the psyche Zoo to home. Elsewhere the mirror of my dresser reads: Women of the World Unite.

This being a gift from Peggy, an ex-Zoo mate. Next year I'll be eighteen, legally a woman and finally free.

Dad knocks on the door. "Jean's here."

"Tell her to wait a second!"

For now, I snap the notebook shut.

||||||||||||||||||||||||||||||||||||||||||||||||||||||||||||||||||||||||||||||||||||||||||||||||||||||||||||||||||||||||||||||||||||||||||||||||||||||||||||||||||||||||||||||||||||||||||

The psychedelic "Slasher" is a lush glimpse of Vietnam-era Phoenix, mental illness and anguish, and the wildness of the Hollywood runaway dream. The girl with a purple flower painted on her cheek and a razor taped behind her ear ...

— REBECCA BYRKIT, Author of *As Larks Stalk the Moonworn Dusks*

Finding My Voice

WENDY PETERS

I cannot recall everything about the events that occurred in March of 1990. I do remember that it was unseasonably warm and that my friends, my brother, and I played in the woods behind my house. We would walk through the wide open field at the end of our street, down a thickly wooded path that wound through the steep hills, and eventually amble down to the creek. It was a magical place where I would rather be than anywhere else in the world. I still dream of dipping my bare feet into the chilly waters. We spent our days scaling the rocks in Beaver Creek, once following it so far that we had to call my mother from a pay phone at a local store a few miles from home. Mom came and collected us in our sopping wet clothes, scolded us for getting into the creek in the winter, knowing good and well that we would do it again the next day. One day Mom took us to the local mall. A reporter there asked if she could do an interview about what we had been doing during our days off from school, to which I replied, "Playing in the woods!" I had no idea that what was going on would have a major impact on my future.

In 1990, I was an awkward 12-year-old girl. I had a head full of permed brown hair, bright green eyes, and a mouth full of braces with those silly neon bands. I had friends, but I was not the most popular girl in my seventh grade class. I loved learning and books, but I hated school because of the teasing that I endured, so of course I was delighted when my teachers decided to take an 11-day hiatus from their jobs to fight for public education.

That is all that I can really recall from the West Virginia teachers' strike of 1990. I just knew that my teachers weren't working. Little did I know that I would be involved in a similar fight 28 years later and that the experiences that I had endured as a self-conscious young girl would help me find my strength to stand up for others. I had no idea that my friend and mentor, Marie Hamrick, was standing with a bullhorn, outside of the state Capitol, organizing teachers from all over the state and that one day I would be following in her footsteps, leading a caravan of teachers and service personnel from my county up Interstate 77 to speak to our elected officials.

During those awkward years in junior high school, I would beg my mother to let me stay home. She would try to encourage me. She, too, had endured teasing in school. She told me that one day I would rise above it, that the people who mistreated others probably felt bad about themselves. Just like many girls that age, I felt that I was the only person in the world that had ever been tormented by their peers. The constant bullying took a toll on my self-esteem. It took many years for me to realize that often those that bully have something or someone hurting them. As the old saying goes, "hurt people hurt people."

As I entered high school, most of the bullying subsided. My chief tormentor moved away and several of the others dropped out of school. My mother was right, of course, just like mothers usually are. Things did get better. I graduated from high school and then college, and I ended up moving into a house less than a mile from the place I grew up. I returned to the community that I swore I wanted to be as far away from as I could get. I now teach in the elementary school that I attended as a child. It turns out that I have been able to use my past experiences to help my students and to help others in my community. Southern West Virginia is my home. A home that throughout the years I have had a love/hate relationship with, but to be perfectly honest, I mostly love this place and the people who live here.

As the cold months began to creep into late 2017, I started to reflect on my life. I needed a change. My husband is a chemist at an environmental testing company and we have a five-year-old son. Discussions began at home about what would be best for our family. I complained that my work as the Raleigh County Education Association president was becoming futile. No one seemed to care anymore. People were apathetic. We would hold meetings and the same ten people would come. The Public Employee Insurance Agency (PEIA) that insured the state workers of West Virginia had just held their public hearings, which very few people attended.

Large increases in premiums and co-pays along with new measures that would base our insurance costs on our total family income would leave my family paying at least an extra 200 dollars a month.

A new app, called Go 365, would require us to play games with our smartphones in order to keep from paying an additional deductible. WV teachers' salaries stood at 48th in the nation. Teachers could go across the border to neighboring states and make 5,000 to 10,000 more dollars a year than in our home state. Over 700 teacher vacancies in the state have left the public schools in a crisis. Teacher colleges in the state were not producing graduates to fill the vacancies and most who did graduate were leaving the state. Who could blame them? I totally understood why they would leave. My family was planning an escape ourselves. What kind of education would my son receive, especially if there were no qualified teachers?

On January 15th, 2018 our state organization, the West Virginia Education Association, was planning a rally at the Capitol. I created a Facebook event and invited all of our local members. We planned to meet at the mall and travel to the Capitol together. When I arrived at the mall, there were three people there to meet us and about 100 people at the rally. I told my friend John Quesenberry on the way home that I was bailing out. I would not seek reelection as the president of my local, and I was probably moving to another state anyway. I just wanted to teach and spend time with my boys. On the way home I stopped into a local store. A teacher there mentioned to me that our unions didn't ever do anything. That was all I needed to hear. I drove home crying. I was giving up. No one else cared, so why should I?

The next week, something changed. I began to receive calls, texts, and messages that people were upset about our insurance. I spoke with the members of our executive committee and the leadership of the county American Federation of Teachers (AFT) and service personnel associations. They were hearing the same things: people were tired of their insurance going up, causing their pay to go down. We had not had a decent raise in years. People were fed up. So we decided that we would have a meeting. If people were really that concerned, then they would show up. We decided to have it in the cafeteria at Woodrow Wilson High School. To my surprise, about 200 people came. We tried to get information out to folks and a few loud and angry people at this point were ready to go on strike.

Dale Lee, our state West Virginia Education Association (WVEA) president, was hearing the same buzz all over the state. It was the perfect storm. The insurance, the low pay, legislation attacking public employees and a Facebook page that was stirring people up were all factors in fueling the fire. The teachers and service personnel of West Virginia were definitely on fire and I had about 1500 angry and scared people in Raleigh County looking to me for guidance. I thank God that he gave me a supportive husband and mother to take care of my son, because the nine-day strike that ultimately ensued were some of the hardest days of my life.

Once beginning the hard work of making change, I had never been so tired in my entire life. I was mentally and physically exhausted. Delegate Ricky Moye, who is a dear friend, would let us rest in his office and would feed us while we were at the Capitol. He had a small love seat in the corner of his office. I would often fall asleep there if I sat down for any length of time. My back and shoulders ached. I literally felt the weight of the world on my shoulders, or at least the weight of about 1500 employees and their families from Raleigh County.

After a late and very eventful Saturday night in the legislature, I came home to rest the next day, which was a Sunday. My mother had been keeping my son while I was in Charleston and my husband was at work.

I would either wake up at 4:30 a.m. to drive the hour to Charleston or I would stay with a childhood friend who lived a block from the Capitol. Mom brought my son home to me that morning so that I could see him.

I held him in my lap as I talked to my husband and my mother. I began to check my messages on my phone as I often had to do. I was inundated with calls, texts, and messages. I could barely keep up. Some of the messages were encouraging, some were folks letting me know what they thought I needed to be doing, and some were just from angry people who did not agree with what we were trying to accomplish. I scrolled through the messages and was surprised when I saw that in my inbox I had a message from someone I had not heard from in ages. I had received a very nasty message from a childhood friend.

The words stung as I read them. I thought to myself, "how dare she?" I had not heard from her or seen her in years. She had no idea what I was going through. She had accused me of being one-sided and not being respectful of others' opinions. I showed it to my mother and began to sob uncontrollably. This old friend's words were not really any different from others who had criticized me, but they were the straw that broke the camel's back. All of the criticism, anger, and hate that had been spewed in my direction had come to a head. It was too much to endure, so I finally did what I should have done all along and cried out to God.

The situation had become bigger than me, bigger than my colleagues, and even bigger than my state and the 55 counties who stood strongly together. I called my close friend Sarita Beckett and told her that the fighting had to stop. It wasn't working. We had to take a different approach. She agreed to help me lead the crowd in prayer the next day.

My husband stayed home with my little boy and my mother went with me to the Capitol that next day. We had spread the word through email and text that we were going to gather at a certain time and pray. I do not think that it was coincidental that a group of students had also planned to surround the outside of the Capitol to pray.

Sarita, our friend Zanetta, and another lady whom I do not know, joined me in the center of the Capitol beneath the rotunda. We took each other's hands and bowed our heads. We lifted up our prayers to God. I can't remember exactly what was said, but I do remember how I felt. I could feel God's presence as others throughout the Capitol joined hands and prayed with us. I truly believed that no matter what happened we would all be all right. We then marched arm in arm up the winding marble steps to the next floor singing "We Shall Overcome." We sat down in front of the looming chamber doors, with arms still linked, in silence. For a moment the chanting stopped. Silence filled the halls, if only for a brief moment. Then, the crowd roared again and the fight continued on for the day.

I can picture it in my mind what God must have seen and heard looking down from the heavens on the people of West Virginia that day. Children and their families encircling the building, hand in hand, praying for those inside, while the people who had always taken care of their children banded together on the inside, hand in hand, crying out to God for mercy and justice.

I remember walking out of the Capitol. It was unseasonably warm, reminding me of a day about 28 years ago. This time, though, that young girl who was so unsure of herself was gone. Now, I was a 41-year-old mother and wife with bright green eyes, laugh lines and streaks of gray in my dark brown hair. I stood at the top of the Capitol steps and looked out into the crowd at all of the people that I loved and cared about and soaked in the warm sun.

Peters captures the stress, tension, and unpleasantness of the first statewide teachers' strike and what it evoked for her, her family, and others. Her detailed description, personal courage, and honesty are hallmarks in this essay.

— **PHYLLIS WILSON MOORE**, Poet and Author

Suite of Five Poems

GRACE CAVALIERI

‖‖

Let's Not Shoot the Poets

they fish at night
and dig by day
they were not born for death
their heavens are low enough to touch
flashing illumination and desire

they make spring beautiful
They listen in their heads
for autumn's breaking
they create and work
turning deadwood to life

society's not enough
so they fly above
its deception and
crash into clouds of meaning

the bucolic would not
exist but for their masterpiece

hostile fire, stay
away from the crush
of boats crowding
the shore—filled

with possible poets –

They are like wild animals
birthing but never forgetting
their loss   Poems
may be crushed but memory
is the hot gold made every day
They stay

In Every Dream An Orphan Builds A House

In each room there is a stone that glows a name
Detour to the hall where Truth is stacked like building blocks
Down the hall are pictures on the wall, each child's face is shown
The cats lie sleeping fat from touch
The dogs bound outside without a leash
Every day is a different color. Grey has been removed
 from the earth back where it belongs
The orphans no longer have to paint houses with their sticks of red and
blue
They no longer need to imagine.

This Poem is Asking for Your Love

This poem is not usually like this
I don't know what came over it
It's mostly violet under the sun
with a large yellow parasol and a pond
with a center that never freezes
I swear I had no idea
I'm so used to trees of hearts and
cherries within its branches
I can't imagine
what woke this poem up
with a truth I never wanted
It called out the tower window and said
I was alone
That in itself is a morbid lie
I have long shadows in Autumn and clouds
anytime there is a sky
In fact everything was going so well until
this poem wanted to undress me
and bring back my love
and hold me close and rub
my forehead when I had fever
It had no idea what trouble could come
from this so I wrote it
then I ran from it
now I can erase it
to show I never needed it after all
because don't you know, Poem,
if you have to *ask* for something
it's no gift.

Come to a Wedding

It's remarkably astonishing
to be with each other
if you try—try to be
unassailable
not successful
that's what others think of you
know what you are / were/ could be
They will now make wedding cakes
and not turn you away
laugh yourself
across the room and yes they changed
because it was meaningful (not useful)
when I don't want anything   I get something
now I want you—all of you
to celebrate
They're making wedding rings
and not turning you away
nothing may be all right for others
but for us nothing
but the best will do
and I (not Uncle Sam!) want you
to party   It used to be bad
bad as a dollar which costs five
I know some things about them
(but just what they are I do not know)
so let them go
and on sheerest ground
warm as flowers opening on
earth sad and real as young girls
once growing old with books unopened

and letters left unread now we can
go on
come on down
up to the future
guess what word I can say
you
Oh unconquerable beauties
talking to the air
indenture yourself
come to the wedding

come to our wedding

Who We Are

"The cry did knock/against
my very heart..." The Tempest

When
we do not feed the hungry children in Biafra
looking at tourists taking their pictures,
then we are the camera.
We are also the neighbor
in West Virginia who shot his cat.
See our hands on the trigger, no matter the gun.
We are the karmic seeds of Viet Nam
running ablaze with fire on our backs.
We're the hummingbird
flying the Atlantic in March.
Now we are Katrina
because clothes were soaked, and when
there were no more, when no help came,
we were the empty verbs.
These are the tears that come for Mozambique,
Its children in the trees,
waiting for rescue helicopters. All this,
when there were other possibilities.
Don't you feel the heartbeat
of the earth, the knob we could turn,
the magical tree we could put back
in the rain forest? Can you count
the number of women sold to slavery
we could wrap
in warm cotton and bring back home?
Riding an idea is like riding the wind

unless we harness
its lonely tumult.
We are the sun on the cold hungry dog
in the streets of Chile,
the disfigured man in prison,
the mass deaths in Bosnia,
their thunderstorms.
We are the shame of the soldier who thought he should
die instead of his buddy. We are the broken clock of
the widows of war.
their last dreams filled with absence—
Since we are the ones who did not feed, comfort or save—
       we are the grave.

Grace Cavalieri's poems are that insistent voice in the back of your mind, the one
that tells you what you already know, what you can't deny any longer. She says
look, here is the wounded, lovely body of the world. Take it in your arms. It's not
too late to feed, to comfort, to save.

                          — VAL NIEMAN, Author of *Leopard Lady*

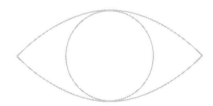

Life Among the Celebrities

REBECCA KIMMONS

Greta Garbo meets Marlon Brando at last when they are sophomores in high school. Greta had seen Marlon in the hallways a year before, always in motion, blue eyes ablaze with something like glee, or mischief, or both. Marlon has a lot going for him. He is already head cheerleader at Warren G. Harding High School. Everybody knows him. He makes everybody happy when he turns his highbeam blues on them. He can make anybody laugh, even the sourest old puss of a teacher. He's the best looking guy in the whole town and everybody knows it.

Greta is pretty, very pretty, but not without flaw. She never smiles because she doesn't want her dark, crooked teeth to show. But that's all right. She is so very pretty in her sad, wan way that she doesn't need to smile. They don't want her to smile. It might mar the perfect symmetry of her face. The porcelain skin might shatter. She doesn't need to be the life of the party anyway. Her sister Lucille Ball will handle all that. Lucille, with her big copper hair and her lust, busting out of every pore. Her big googly blue eyes and her bouncing breasts, always waiting to bounce, always wanting, wanting to bounce.

And if you forget Greta's mother, then you're missing a big part of the story. Queen Elizabeth, Princess Grace, who else? Lillian Roth, for sure, right down to Dirty Lil. You better not forget her. Marlene Dietrich.

Getting married is an important thing to do. There they are, Greta and Marlon, standing at the brink of their lives in that August during the war, Greta picturing herself queen of something one day, and Marlon wanting only to possess Greta.

On the day before the wedding, Marlon's family arrives from West Virginia. The scene of the wedding is the little industrial town of Odawa, Michigan, which is very much like the little industrial town of Beckham, West Virginia with its big, square, official court house building at the center, and unassuming little houses for workers lined up in rows all around, except for the big fine houses on avenues named Forestlawn or Fairhaven, where the bosses and business owners live. Greta is working that summer in Odawa as a curb girl to pay for her stylish wedding. She has just turned eighteen, and she insists that it all be perfect. Marlon is coming in on leave from the Navy. He is eighteen, too. He wants war as badly as he wants Greta.

Mr. and Mrs. Brando drive north on winding roads for nearly three days to arrive in Odawa. They bring along Betty Grable, their eldest daughter, who will be the matron of honor. There is no way that Lucille Ball could ever play that role. Betty's husband of six or seven years, Burt Lancaster with a purple birthmark covering half his face, does not attend the wedding.

When they get to Odawa, the Brandos check into the very best suite at the MoonGlo Motel, where all out-of-town guests are staying, courtesy of Mr. Cary Grant, who owns it. Mr. Grant has a special relationship with Marlene, Greta's mother. In the early morning hours of the day of the wedding, Mr. Brando saw Marlene leave Mr. Grant's room, dressed only in a towel.

The wedding goes off without a hitch. Greta is sad that she gave herself up to Marlon the day before. Now she knows that she does not want to marry him. She is sad and sorry. She tells him she does not want to marry. Now she regrets that, too. In the wedding pictures her doleful eyes look toward nothing, her sad and beautiful mouth is poised in wistful perfection. One side of Marlon's mouth tilts up in a half-smile, the other tilts down. In his wounded eyes is a glint of death.

After the wedding Marlon goes back to the Navy, back to Drake Island, back to the war that is now one month over, leaving him to do nothing more than type forms. He has not killed any Japs. He has not tasted any blood. Greta goes back to Beckham to live with the Brandos until Marlon comes home.

Months go by, and Marlon gets no letters from Greta. Hadn't he just married in August? It's September, then October, then November, and still no letters. He writes to her every day at first, then every week, then every day again in a flurry of rage, and then he quits. He will be going home in June, and he will know then why there are no letters. No letters from her.

There are letters from others. Marlon's brother, Buster Keaton, writes to report the unsettling news that Greta sometimes does not come home immediately after school. Their sister Ingrid Bergman watches Greta, and listens. Dad Brando watches and listens, too. Dad Brando can see Marlene in the girl Greta's every move. He savors the delicious prospect of her inevitable fall. He watches and waits.

Burt Lancaster stops by the Brando house every day as a matter of course. Burt and Betty live a quarter-mile away in the swampy bottomland of the creek, in a house Burt built for Betty on the Ace's land. A dense patch of woods separates the two houses, Burt and Betty's in the bottom, and the Ace's at the top of the hill. Dad Brando is the Ace. His is the power and the glory.

Jenny Lind, Marlon's mother, watches Greta, and she watches everyone else, too. Her favorite post is the kitchen sink, where a window without curtains offers a splendid view of Dr. Lillian Gish's house. Jenny's dark eyes know the inside of Dr. Gish's house very well. Its windows, flounced with ruched organza, framing a world of polished silver, Persian carpets and silk damask upholstery. Dr. Gish, a widow, lives there with her four daughters, Meg, Jo, Beth, and Amy. Sometimes Jenny lives there, too, in her head.

Sometimes Greta walks home from school with Beth. She wishes she could keep on walking beyond the house so full of watchful Brandos. She happily would turn in with Beth to the place where all is quiet, all is beautiful and calm, all is serenely happy. Marlon is gone, except for the letters. The letters that come every day. She doesn't open them. She is ashamed that she has not written to him. Not one letter.

She could never tell him what has happened. And she could never talk to him and not tell him. She says nothing.

Burt is long, lithe, and strong, a working man of twenty-eight or thirty, in his prime. The purple birthmark makes one side of his face look like a mask, and at first, Greta is afraid to look at him. Once he starts talking to her, she sees that his eyes search her face, looking hard to see what she thinks of his face. Greta is careful not to register anything. Just because his face is disfigured doesn't mean he shouldn't get a chance. Greta is horrified. Her, a married woman, and him, her brother-in-law. A chance? A chance at what?

Burt is the only one who really talks to Greta now that she is part of the Brando household. He is nice to her when he comes around. The conversation isn't about anything much, but he is warm. He's a foreman in the mines, working what he calls the hoot-owl shift, but she never sees him dirty. When he comes by the house he is always clean and well-dressed, and he smells good. Sometimes, in the afternoons before anyone else gets home, while Betty's at the beauty shop, Greta and Burt sit on the front porch and talk. Every now and then they talk about the Ace. Burt can talk to the Ace. Greta doesn't. She watches the Ace every morning and every evening at the table, how he treats everybody mean but Baby. She tells Burt about the snort, how the Ace takes the first and biggest portion of all the food, and then fills up Baby's plate. Then he snorts and says, go on and eat. Maybe he doesn't really snort. Maybe she just sees it.

There is young Buster Keaton, and budding Ingrid Bergman, and Baby. Buster sleeps at the top of the ladder, in the attic he once shared with Marlon. Ingrid has the room downstairs with the latticed porch, and Baby has the big room with the bath. Greta tucks herself onto the daybed of the apartment that never was an apartment because Jenny can't take the smell of another female in her house, except for, maybe, her daughters. Now there is Greta.

Greta pokes around at the Kandy Korner until closing time, then she takes her books and walks alone in the twilight, under the street lights on West Main Street. The street will soon plunge from the ridgetop over the mountain, bucking and twisting down the steep hillside. Marlon's face flashes before her, as true as on a movie screen. Of course he is laughing. Assbuster Hill, he is saying. She laughs inside her head, her face never moving.

In a moment, car lights fall on her, making her squint. A car is coming up Assbuster Hill. The car slows and the driver rolls down the window. It's Burt, driving his big black Mercury Eight. "Hop in, angel face," he says. "I'll give you a ride home," even though he is going in the wrong direction. His voice is sure and pleasant.

Greta is in no hurry to get back to the Brandos where she knows there will be a sink full of dirty dishes, but she gets into the car anyway, sinking down into its plushy seat. The blue, golden and green lights on the dashboard of the new Mercury vaguely illuminate Burt's face. He says he swung around to pick up Betty at the beauty shop, but she has bookkeeping to do.

I could help with the bookkeeping, Greta says, you know that's what I'm taking in school. She sits with her hands folded in her lap. She shudders slightly when she thinks about the dirty jokes and the filthy language that spew out of Betty's mouth every time she opens it. She wishes she really wanted to help Betty but she doesn't like her. She likes bookkeeping even less.

You're out kind of late, ain't you? Burt says.

Is it late? Greta says, ignoring the darkness that means it is easily past six. She wonders why he insists on saying ain't when he drives this big fine car. Ignorant, she thinks, and instantly is sorry. She shouldn't be so unkind.

The Ace will be wondering where you are, Burt says. He laughs a little. They both know what that means.

Greta says nothing, but she can see Burt's profile faintly etched in the light of the dashboard. There is no birthmark now, only the perhaps elegant thrust of his nose, a line that might be called beautiful. Had she noticed this before? There is a glint of gold reflected in his eye. The hot smell of her now floods the car, and she feels very uneasy and she doesn't know why, except that she does know why.

Burt has driven to the grounds of the drive-in movie theater. Everything is dark now on the top of the hill on an autumn school night. He turns off the motor and the car lights. He looks at Greta, then reaches out to touch her hand, lightly.

You're in no hurry to get home, he says. She says nothing, but her insides burst into flame. He watches her for a moment. She wonders what he will say next.

I hate what they're doing to you, he says. The two sit silently in the car for a few moments, and then he says, I see how they treat you, always watching you. He cocks his head a little sideways. His face is mostly hidden in the dark, but she can feel his eyes. They're like hands, moving all around her face. I see how he watches you, Burt says, and I know what he's watching for.

Greta feels like a bird in a box. Honey. Angel face. She tries to catch her breath. She might not be able to breathe. This that is about to happen has happened before, when her Uncle Tyrone Power picked her up after school in his new car. Should she scream? No, no, she should not scream. She should just relax. Relax. She turns her face toward him. She can barely see him, but she can feel him breathing. She can taste tobacco, and maybe alcohol. Is it beer? I see how miserable you are, angel, he says. She feels that she can't move. He reaches out and puts his hand gently on the bare flesh under her skirt, just above her knee. His hand is warm, and surprisingly soft. I don't like the way they treat you at all, he says. His hand is gentle, just barely touching her flesh.

She looks at him without seeing him now, wondering what exactly will happen next, how and at what moment. She feels hot and angry and thirsty and hungry and mad. And hungry. What is he watching for,

Greta hears herself say. She sounds small, like someone very far away. She feels Burt looking at her. She feels the space between them close. He's watching, he says, low and quiet, for this. He leans into her, his hand lightly sliding up and inside her thigh, his mouth closing in on hers.

The house sits dark and silent as Greta approaches it, walking along the sidewalk, feeling the moonless pull of the stream that snakes through the trees between Burt and Betty's and the Brandos'. A street lamp casts enough light for her to make her way down the steps from the sidewalk to the latticed porch well below the street, mostly hidden from view. Greta takes her saddle oxfords off when she gets to the porch, and eases the door open to the room where Ingrid lies in her bed with her eyes closed. Greta is relieved when the door makes no noise. She tiptoes across the room in her sock feet, toward the room where the daybed waits. Everything is dark except for Greta's insides. They are flaming white hot, melting everything from her brain to her bottom. She feels slightly sick but still hungry. Even hungrier now. She feels disgust. And hunger. She lies down and without taking off her clothes, pulls the covers up over her face. Tears squeeze out of her tight-shut eyes, slide down her cheeks and plunk down onto the pillow.

The morning sun comes clamoring in through the blinds that bang over the big double kitchen windows, lighting up the table with its unbearable bright yellow sunniness. The Ace is in his seat, presiding over the bacon and biscuits with Baby at his side. Buster and Ingrid are in their places on the board over the window radiator, their seats. Greta climbs the back stairs up to the kitchen, her freshly scrubbed face carefully composed. Jenny is pouring hot gravy from the big iron skillet onto everyone's plates. The Ace is muttering a little tune of his own. Hot gravy, hot gravy, he sings, as if to himself, and nods toward Greta. Get you a biscuit, honey, he says. Jenny, get the girl some gravy. Greta sits down at the table, and Jenny sets a plate in front of her, and the Ace hands her a biscuit. Jenny ladles a big slop of hot gravy on it with a deft hand. Once the Ace digs in, everyone else begins to eat. Eggs and bacon, biscuits and gravy. The room is quiet except for the clank of silverware on plates. The Ace picks up his coffee cup and nods at Jenny. She picks up the pot from the stove, and wheels around to pour the Ace another cup. She moves like a cat.

Ace begins to sing another little tune, but this time it's a song everybody knows, a jumping little song that gets played over and over again on the jukebox at the Kandy Korner. *Don't sit under the apple tree with anyone else but me, no, no, no,* he sings, *doodle de do,* then he looks out over the table, meeting Buster's eye. Buster laughs and Ingrid looks sideways at the Ace and then at Buster, and she laughs, too. Then they all look down at their plates. When Greta looks up, her eyes meet the Ace's. His hands and cup cover most of his face, except for his eyes. They are Marlon's eyes, full of glee, or mischief, or both.

That afternoon, Greta skips the Kandy Korner and hurries back to the Brando house while the afternoon sun is still shining. She washes the breakfast dishes, she sweeps the floor, she tidies up the house before going downstairs to the room where she sleeps. Mom and Dad Brando are still at the store. Buster will be coming in at any minute, then Ingrid and Baby. They all would be here soon. She settles down with her books. In a moment, she hears a noise at the door. It isn't exactly knocking, but it's definitely a noise. She gets up to see what it is, and there is Burt, trying the door. It's fastened with a simple latch and it gives just enough resistance for Greta to see who it is.

Open the door, Burt whispers.

(None of this actually happened. No one really knows what happened. There are several different stories. Greta and Marlon are dead. So are Burt and Betty, and Ingrid. Buster died first, more than twenty-five years ago.)

Marlon sails into the Port of New York late one June afternoon, one of thousands of sailors coming home. As soon as he can, he catches a southbound train. It chugs down through Washington D.C. and on through Virginia all that night. At dawn, the train crosses into West Virginia at the old Sulphur Springs. It comes into the New River Gorge at Hanson Depot at half past seven and by eight forty-one, just a little over an hour later, Marlon jumps off the train at Stokes, into the steaming jungle of a West Virginia morning. A cab is waiting for nobody in particular. Marlon hops in, and away they go, on a Tuesday morning with the bugs screaming and birds screeching, up the steep and winding road to Beckham.

It's around nine-thirty when the cab pulls up in front of Two-Twenty-Two Illyria Street. Marlon jumps out of the taxi, grabs his duffel bag, and jumps like a cat over the sidewalk to the steps below. In a bound or two, he is on the latticed porch. Nobody is home but the door is open. He walks into the morning twilight. The air is thick and sweet with the smell of female. His sister Ingrid's bed is unmade. When his eyes adjust, he forges on into the apartment where he sees Greta's stuff. Her panties washed and hanging on a rack to dry. A stack of letters on the floor beside the vanity. He picks the letters up and looks at them. Not one had been opened. He takes her panties off the rack and wipes his face and mouth, then throws them on the floor.

Greta knows he will be home sometime soon. She can hardly think of anything else. She thinks about it but she doesn't really think about it. It's a low-grade buzz in her brain all morning and all afternoon as she enters numbers in one place, then again in another, and writes Dear Mr. So and So, I'm writing to tell you goodbye. No, no, that wouldn't be the best way to say it. Was he back yet? Where would he be this afternoon when she got home? She couldn't picture him at all.

After school, instead of heading for Two-Twenty-Two Illyria Street, she walks uptown. She watches her saddle oxfords stepping along the sidewalk toward the Kandy Korner. She watches herself push the door in, and turns toward the soda fountain.

There is Marlon, sitting on a stool, watching her come through the door. She says nothing. He watches her face and it registers nothing. Her face is exactly the same as when he left. A picture of alabaster purity.

You're home, she says, after a moment.

Here is Marlon before her. His unforgettable blue eyes which she had forgotten. Marlon was back. She breathes him in like a drug.

He laughs and his voice sounds the same. She looks warily into his eyes. He doesn't flinch. You look wonderful, he says. He means it, too. The translucence of her skin, the caramel color of her hair curling on her shoulders slays him, as always.

Let's get out of here, he says. He slides off the stool and walks past her, heading toward the door. When she just stands there, he turns, and takes her hand.

||||||||||||||||||||||||||||||||||||||||||||||||||||||||||||||||||||||||||||||||||||||||||||||||||||||||||||||||||||||||||||||||||||||||||||||||||||||||||||||||||||||||||||||||||||||||||||||

On one level, this story is a realistically told account of a wartime bride living uncomfortably among her absent husband's family. But it is also an intriguing postmodern tale which, drawing attention to itself as a story, causes us to think about narrative itself.

— **MICHELE SCHIAVONE**, Professor Emeritus, Editor

Empowerment

DALEEN R. BERRY

||||||||||||||||||||||||||||||||||||||||||||||||||||||||||||||

The day my husband died I was wearing a cotton gown, positioning my arm just so, while medical technicians performed an ultrasound on my right breast. When the two techs left me alone to confer with the radiologist, I received the impersonal call about his unexpected death. They returned moments later, to find me doubled over, sobbing incoherently.

For more than a year I fumbled around. Stumbled, really, through a fog of grief that paralyzed me one day and sent me running for comfort the next. When I realized the only way I could function was to objectively don my investigative reporter's hat, I went to work, methodically sorting and itemizing the things he left behind. Papers and emails and text messages, and bid sheets and signed contracts and receipts, all in preparation for what was to come.

What was to come led me to months of researching, reading, and analyzing—dates, places, names and numbers. I followed the money trail as far as I could. Then, after doing all the work I was humanly capable of, I sat down and surrendered.

Surrendered to the realization that I was losing my home.

They say we are a litigious society.

In this case, "they" are insurance companies intent on capping damages in what has become a tort reform war, making it more difficult for people who have suffered real harm to sue.[4] Or, all too often, to be adequately compensated for their injuries. As a journalist, I've spent years telling people who claim Americans are sue happy that such stuff and nonsense is well-aimed propaganda—from corporations hoping to minimize their own losses.[5] Big businesses who spend millions, if not billions, in advertising designed to fool the American public.

Still, the most oft-cited case in support of the "sue happy" argument is *Liebeck v. McDonald's Restaurants*. Its name comes from Stella Liebeck, the 79-year-old widow whose scalding hot coffee burned her so badly at a drive-through window that she required two years of surgeries to repair the damage done to her pelvic area.

Of course, that's the bit we didn't hear about in the news. It probably wasn't headline worthy. Nor did we learn that Liebeck offered to settle for $20,000, but when McDonald's refused to pay more than $800, she had no choice but to sue.[6] Even then, we only heard about the $2.86 million civil judgment, leading to collective public outrage. Not how the judge in that case reduced her award to $640,000.[7]

My surrender involved turning the entire behemoth of my late husband's business materials over to attorneys who got involved. After twelve, sixteen, even twenty-hour days organizing all the evidence, it felt so good just to let it all go. To take a break from a process that had utterly consumed me.

Except taking a break was not exactly good for me. Nor was relinquishing the reins on a legal issue that I knew more about than any ten people combined. It felt like giving up—like I was giving up on him. On the man who made a point to provide for me in his Last Will and Testament, by leaving me a home. This home, which the attorneys were trying to take.

I never wanted to file a lawsuit. But after becoming administratrix of my late husband's estate, I soon learned there was no other way. What do you do, when someone who has stolen an entire company valued at more than $1 million, as well as the land that company sits on—refuses to admit he stole a single dime? Who comes to the table under the guise of settling, but only if you let him continue taking what is yours?

Or in this case, what now belongs to the estate? The estate, which doesn't just have one heir—me—but which has three other heirs, all his minor grandchildren. Including the oldest one, whom I have known since infancy, having been a family friend long before I became his wife.

He didn't leave anything to their parents, his children, and it's taken me awhile to remember why. To recall the conversations we had when he was drawing up his will, since I then found his decision quite odd. And I distinctly remember asking if they would feel like he was cutting them out. He assured me they wouldn't, because he had given them tremendous monetary help, long after they became adults. And, as he said, his grandchildren's parents were financially secure.

I heard what he left unsaid: there were other people who could influence his adult children. People who might negatively impact his grandchildren's inheritance—which he didn't want to happen.

On some level, though, I also know he felt guilty. Before I agreed to marry him, less than two years after his first wife succumbed to cancer, I insisted on his children's blessing. Or else we would wait, I told them all. In spite of their seemingly sincere protests at the time, that it wasn't too soon for him to remarry, they quickly asserted squatters' rights, and interfered with our marriage for fifteen long years.

His guilt was due to the problems that ensued. For the toll it took on our marriage. On me. On us.

How little they knew.

How much less they understand.

In a weirdly macabre case of déjà vu, one year later I was in the same exam room, wearing yet another cotton gown, repeating those identical diagnostic steps. Except then, no one called to relay such devastating news. The news from the ultrasound results—"We need to do a biopsy"—was bad enough.

For six months, two weeks, and one day, I awoke each morning to the taste of fear. Fear that the mass in my right breast would turn malignant from extreme stress, as I do battle with men in suits, lawyers acting on behalf of the man who wants to steal my home.

A man who is using the judicial system to do so. Because my home is not only part of the estate—it's part of the contract that led to the theft—and thus, the lawsuit itself.

I have no money: His income once supported us both. Even though I churned out seven books in six years, my income wasn't enough for one person, let alone two. But most of his income was stolen, long before he died in 2017, leaving me to carry on his fight. For a time, that fight included living without a kitchen or a shower, so I ate foods that required no cooking and bathed at the gym, reduced to poverty I hadn't known since childhood.

One such daunting battle could fell any of us, but since 2016 I've faced three others: searching for my daughter, presumed missing, on the other side of the continent; suddenly and unexpectedly losing my husband; and watching my sister succeed in having my mother declared incompetent, which tore our already frayed family to tatters.

All formidable battles in and of themselves, but completely unlike the current legal one. Having no money makes it all but impossible to hire an attorney. So, to quote John, Paul, George and Ringo, I asked for "a little help from my friends." The crowdsourcing money I raised was enough to file one motion, and not much more.

But then, frighteningly, I learned that my attorney held some extremist political views. An avid Trump supporter, his Facebook page told the tale. There, he shared conspiracy theory rants from Alex Jones' Infowars, such as the one about Parkland High School student David Hogg. "He looks like the devil," my attorney wrote.

How, I wondered, as I read those words with growing horror, could I possibly trust a man with such fanatical leanings to adequately represent my best interests in a court of law? In the end, I couldn't.

By then, it didn't matter anyway. The crowdsourcing money was gone. Every law firm I called or visited said the same thing: they either had a conflict, due to the parties in the case, or they wanted somewhere between a $5,000 and $25,000 retainer. A seasoned lawyer has since told me that those high quotes are basically code for "I don't want your case."

Legal agencies designed to help the poor—in this case, me—apparently do not handle dead people's estates. Or real estate matters. I know this because I've contacted them all. Perhaps they don't take on such cases because, in theory, anyone who has an estate or owns land and assets should have the monetary resources to hire an attorney.

I've often found the theory of law to be in stark contrast with reality. Many times over the years, I've met people who can't afford legal counsel. Most of them are women. Personally, I've been disenfranchised in just such a way more times than I care to recall. For instance, when my first husband sued for custody of our four children, six years after our divorce was final. Or when a landlord failed to make repairs to provide my children and me with clean water.

Of those legal battles, the one involving my children's safety and well-being carried the potential for the biggest win—or the most destructive loss. For them and for me. This time, though, winning or losing will exact a far heavier monetary price tag. This time, I may lose my home, and the income my late husband intended to leave behind, both for his grandchildren and me. His life insurance, if you will.

So I have no choice but to fight, and that I am. To the death. Ah yes, but whose death? That remains to be seen, but I am determined it won't be mine. Ultimately, I believe, my fight will lead to the death of eleven long years of blatant theft.

Theft which led us to sell almost all our furniture, which led him to tell me we could no longer afford to pay the utilities at our townhouse, so while I was searching for my daughter, he went to stay with his.

Theft which caused him to later ask me to find a full-time job so I could support us both.

Theft which, I now believe, ultimately killed him.

Pro sé is the legal term for people who represent themselves in court. But when you have no money to hire legal counsel, or you can't find an attorney willing to step up to the plate, that old adage, "A person who represents himself has a fool for an attorney" is rather a moot point.

Acting pro sé in this matter is one of the most difficult and challenging ordeals I will ever experience. I know this. How could I not? I sit here surrounded by twelve law books, containing page upon page of case law, state and federal statutes, and definitions for time limits and foreign terms like "de novo," which is Latin for "from new." De novo basically means a court case starts over.

In the space of a few months, as I awaited my follow-up mammogram, I went from feeling completely powerless—like I had no voice and therefore, no choice—to knowing I am competent and capable of doing what I must. That I can help the court understand what's at stake, and convince it that the estate is the only honest and ethical party in this case.

I went from feeling like a marshmallow, or some spineless creature incapable of making any decision, to feeling so empowered that this is no longer about me fighting back. No, this is about the rest of my life, which I suspect may soon include law school. Because in filing an appeal with the state supreme court to try to stop the sale of my home, I'm saying: "I refuse to surrender." That the appellate court has decided to hear my appeal only reaffirms my growing feeling of being unfettered.

To that end, I've taken my home and rearranged its contents to make it mine. Not his. Not ours, but mine. The spare bedroom is once again my workspace, except this time I humorously call it "Daleen's law office." I might even hang up a shingle in the doorway, inscribed with those words. To give me something to aspire to, and to laugh about.

How did I reach this peaceful plateau?

I swam here, doing lap after lap at the gym. I danced here, turning myself loose to pulsating beats while home alone. I read, book after sacred, irreverent, page-turning, book.

And I walked here. Walking through my favorite cemetery on a recent, unseasonably warm winter day, I looked across the mountain ridges and saw two states: Pennsylvania to the north and, to my east, the "Free State of Preston"—Preston County, the place I call home. As I walked, I thought about my new knees, for which I am so very grateful. I jokingly say they're bionic, because after living with debilitating knee pain from the time I was a teenager, and slowly giving up one activity after another, I have given myself a new lease on life.

In May 2015 I endured hours of excruciating pain after having them cut in half with a power saw. Bilateral knee surgery is the official term, which means two knees are replaced simultaneously. But post-surgery, due to a pharmacy error, I spent the entire night without sleep—or a single painkiller.

Morphine was finally delivered to my room at 5 a.m. the next day. I slept for several hours as my husband sat there, religiously pushing the button that would deliver dose after dose of liquid narcotic into my bloodstream, ensuring my body got the sleep it needed to begin healing.

That kind of pain can defeat you—or it can fortify you. Only now do I fully comprehend that it made me stronger, showing me the stuff I was made of.

Am made of.

It's taken me almost two years to finally come to peace. Not with his death, or the lingering essence of him—because, like in the Alison Krauss song, his ghost still haunts this house. But I am at peace with the familial battles that led us here. I am at peace, too, in this home he left behind.

For me—and only me.

||

Daleen Berry's sharp, honest writing had me from the first awful moments of her story, a layer-cake of fear, loss, and disappointment. Facing medical, legal, and financial troubles all at once with little outside help, Berry shoved her desperation aside and did what she does best: putting her investigative skills to work. The resulting empowerment is cheer-worthy, but not surprising. I hope this brilliant woman adds law school to her list of achievements; we all need help sometimes, and I can already imagine having a lawyer named Daleen Berry on my side.

— JANE CONGDON, Author of *How the Wild Effect Turned Me into a Hiker at 69: An Appalachian Trail Adventure*

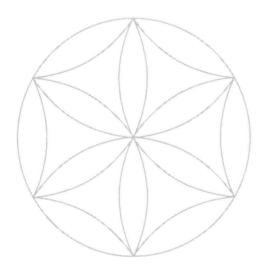

One Dark Night

M. LYNNE SQUIRES

||||||||||||||||||||||||||||||||||||||||||||||||||||||||||||||||||||||

I stood on the front porch, smoking a cigarette. A warm evening, yet I was shivering inside a floor-length fleece robe. Peach, although my roommate insisted it was pink. Across the narrow side yard, the front door of the house next door swung open and four or five young men stumbled out. One spilled beer and the others laughed. A couple of them glanced my way, one raising his chin in a silent hello.

Strangers, all. I wanted to call over for help, or at least for a conversation that would carry me across the yard into the safety of a crowd, however small. I didn't see any women. And I just couldn't trust that being in the company of a handful of men would be safer than being in the company of the one currently inside my own home.

I heard my back door open and the screen door screech across the cracked and tilted concrete stoop. Peering around the house, I saw a shadowy figure run to the alley. That made the decision of talking to the strangers next door a moot point. I flicked my cigarette onto the lawn and watched briefly as the glowing cherry faded to black. Entering the foyer, I shut the door and locked it, and repeated the action with the back door. Returning to the living room, I slid down the wall facing the front door. Tears welled up as I thought about the knock on the door less than an hour before. I lit another cigarette. As I sat on the floor and sobbed, it burned low, dropping ash on the avocado shag carpet.

Heading to work that morning, I had crossed the street from my house to the bus stop, joining a half dozen others. Some nodded or said good morning. A newcomer to our usual morning group of riders smiled and asked if the bus was typically on time. "I don't generally catch the bus at this stop." He appeared to be near my age and told me he worked downtown. He carried on a friendly banter with me till the bus pulled next to the curb. He wished me a nice day and ambled to the rear of the bus. I sat in the front seat and settled in with a book for the trip into town.

I don't remember anything else about the remainder of the day. Not where I was working at the time, nor whom I was working with, or even what time of year it was. It wasn't cold, so it wasn't yet winter. But beyond that, I don't know.

Around 9 that evening, someone knocked on my door. When I answered it, there stood the man who had chatted with me at the bus stop that morning. He explained that he had seen me leave the house this morning, and as he was passing by he thought he would stop and say hello. He said he enjoyed our talk this morning. He pulled out a pack of Kools and after patting his pockets asked if I had a light. I turned and walked into the living room to retrieve a lighter. When I turned back to the door he was standing inside and was closing the front door behind him.

He walked casually to the sofa and sat down. Patting the cushion beside him, he said, "Come sit with me. Let's burn one." He turned the Kool pack upside down and tapped the bottom until a mostly burnt up joint fell into his hand.

"Not much of one, I'd say." I laughed nervously. Not a stranger to pot, but not accustomed to, or comfortable with a perfect stranger making himself comfortable in my living room.

"It will do the trick." He fired up the roach and passed it to me. I took a hit and passed it back. I thought if we finished off the little bit, he'd have a buzz and continue on his way.

Instead, he leaned over close and tried to kiss me. I tried to shove him away. His pleasant demeanor changed in an instant to aggressive and demanding. He stood up and pulled me off of the sofa. "Show me the rest of your place." He pointed to the hallway, and I was too afraid not to do what he said. The first room was my roommate's bedroom. He walked in and told me to sit on the bed. Grabbing some lipstick of her dressing table, he threw it at me. "Here, put some on." When I protested he said, "I don't care what you want. Put it on!"

It felt surreal to be applying orange-red lipstick without the benefit of a mirror and at the command of a stranger. He insisted on seeing the rest of the house and walked me down the hall to the large kitchen in the rear. He walked toward the fridge and I turned and ran into the bathroom, locking the door behind me. To say "locking" seems a bit pretentious. The lock was merely a brass hook inserted into a matching brass eye on the door frame. He tried to open the door, and failing that, demanded that I come out.

The window was large enough to crawl out, had it not been painted shut for years. I looked around for something to use as a weapon. Hairbrush, makeup brush, toothbrush. No, no, and no. The toilet tank cover seemed a possibility. The bathroom was so small, I didn't think I could even manage a decent swing. Before I could remove the lid, I heard a noise at the door. Turning, I saw a thin knife blade slide through the crevice and easily pop the hook from the eye. The door swung open, and now I had a stranger in my house, two feet away and armed with a knife.

He forced me into my bedroom with the knife blade pressed into my neck. What happened next I managed to block out for the most part. I remember thinking I'd need to wash the sheets. I hoped when he was finished he'd just leave and wouldn't steal my tiny trinket box that held my mother's birthstone ring and my fire opal earrings. I alternated between hoping my roommate would stay gone, and hoping for the rescue of her arrival. Afterward, I stumbled off the bed, grabbed my robe and fled to the front porch.

Later that evening, I began packing my belongings. I moved that night and never returned. I didn't call the authorities. I didn't speak of it with anyone.

I didn't dwell on it. I saw TV shows and read articles where other women just couldn't move past what had happened to them. They lived and relived it in the retelling and repeating over and over. They seemed to become prisoners of that single experience, some even to the exclusion of being able to live in the present. They didn't trust men. They didn't enjoy sex. They lost who they were as they lived shrouded in a cloak of pain and shame. Those things were not my experience.

People deal with things differently. I didn't need to relive anything. That moment, that experience wasn't going to define me. Yes, it happened. Yes, it was horrifying. Yes, I threw away the pink-peach robe. I didn't talk with any men I didn't know at bus stops, in elevators, on the street. I didn't open my door blindly. I used better judgment. I also accepted what happened and was grateful for not being injured or killed. Then I moved on.

I was in control of me, of my thoughts and my actions. From that day to this, I have never described myself as a victim. I don't think of myself as a survivor. I was an unwilling participant in a two-person play, performed to an audience of none.

The #metoo movement arrived full force in 2017. I admitted that I too was part of #metoo. I looked around and realized nearly every woman I knew was claiming the hashtag as part of their experience. It was an empowering feeling to know that I was in the company of many, many others. Twitter confirmed over 1.7 million #metoo tweets from 85 countries.

My solitary experience is folded into the experiences of hundreds of thousands of women. From that day to this, I have rebuffed, rejected, and outright shamed men for their uninvited advances, unwanted innuendos, and inappropriate touches. And I am not alone.

Sometimes I remember that night. When I see a peach bathrobe, or when I drive past that house. I no longer remember his face. Now his face is every man, everywhere.

Now I am armed. With words, action, perseverance, resistance. And with my own strength of being, enabled by every woman, everywhere.

A warrior is defined as a person engaged in some sort of struggle or conflict, and I can't think of a more apt description for a woman who has been an "unwilling participant in a two-person play, performed to an audience of none." Women are expected to be nice, courteous. To carry on the conversation at the bus stop. To look for a lighter. Then blamed when those very things lead to unwanted outcomes. The endless litany of why she did or didn't do a thousand other things goes on and on. This is the battle women have been fighting since the dawn of time. It is time we started recognizing our warriors who not only find a way to move beyond what was done to them but also to continue fighting for the luxury of just walking down the street in broad daylight. Alone.

— **MARSHA BLEVINS**, Writer

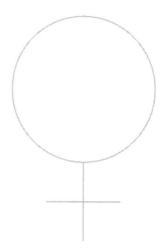

Ready About, Hard Alee

COLLEEN ANDERSON

My house is infested with fleas and I am running the vacuum when, five hundred miles away, my brother—fifty-one, in chronic pain from a work injury, unemployed, and uninsured—shoots and kills himself. When I turn off the vacuum, there are two messages from my mother, in a voice so flat that it clearly means big trouble. *Dad had another stroke*, I think. Then my mother calls for a third time.

It is late July. Somewhere in Ohio, when the West Virginia hills have given way to fields of corn and soybeans, I stop at a farm market where twenty or thirty people are eating hot dogs, burgers, watermelon, and ice cream in the shade underneath a pavilion. Some musicians arrive and play country music. The day is brilliant and sunny, with a nice breeze, the kind of day when my brother would love to be out on the Saginaw Bay in a sailboat, except that he is dead. The living world, the one with tastes and smells and textures, is a transparent film laid over a colorless slab.

I reach Michigan in early evening. My father lies in his recliner. His arms are wrinkled; he resembles a deflated plastic Christmas decoration in someone's lawn. "I was too hard on him," he says.

"Dad, no. He was suffering from depression, and it killed him." Maybe both things are true. My father never mistreated any of us, but the burden of his expectations must have overwhelmed my brother and unlike my father, my brother was not suited to run a business and supervise a dozen employees. He preferred working alone, making something from wood, rewiring a small appliance, hunting in the woods behind his house, or steadying the mainsail as the old Lightning leaned in the wind.

My mother says, "He said he was coming to plant some flowers in that bed beside the house. I knew something terrible had happened when he didn't come. He would never let us down. He always takes such good care of us."

My younger sister, the mystic among us, tells me she dreamed about my brother the night before. In the dream, he was drinking his favorite Scotch whiskey straight from the bottle, holding it up to salute her. "He was letting me know he would be all right," she says. Then she collapses, weeping.

At the funeral, in lieu of a eulogy, I read an essay, written years before—before his injury and the drinking and the depression—about the pleasure of sailing with my brother on Lake Huron, about his methodical grace and easy competence. My father begins to cry, and I have to look away to keep reading.

I drive the car on the way back to my parents' house, along flat roads gridded in one-mile increments. It's another glorious summer day. High clouds move like small craft across the immense Michigan sky.

Our family is a sailboat. My father stands near the mast, ropes in hand, calling out the orders: "Ready about! Hard alee!" My mother is in the cabin, unpacking the picnic lunch, organizing the tidy cabinets. My sister reclines on the bow, gazing across the expanse of the bay. I am at the tiller, pulling it this way and that, trying to keep us on course. But our rudder is gone. My brother—the quiet one, the designated heir to the business, the one who stayed in Michigan, the caretaker—is missing. We are adrift.

Perhaps it begins that day, in the midst of pain and confusion: I begin to comprehend that I will assume the responsibility of the only son in this new family, the one we will have to become without my brother. As my parents grow older, I will be the one to plant flowers and celebrate birthdays with them; to deal with the real estate agents, and then the doctors and hospice nurses. I will be the one holding my mother's hand when she stops breathing. All the sacred privileges and duties will pass to me. I will accept them, resent them, and eventually cherish them.

Slowly, slowly, with tears and arguments, with hugging and laughter, and mostly without mentioning my brother, we will rebuild our vessel. It will be smaller than the old one, but it will float.

|||

Exquisitely painful to read, this short work of creative nonfiction packs powerful emotion into every word. The catastrophic event behind the piece is a brother's suicide, yet Colleen Anderson delivers a full rendering of family dynamics: the before, the after, and even the beyond. She touches on the guilt experienced by all those close to a suicide and the inevitable search for cause. Anderson uses the brother's love for sailing as an extended metaphor for the family, which she compares to a sailboat with the father at the helm giving orders, the mother in charge of food, the sister as a mystic gazing outward, and herself as the tiller trying to hold the family on course—but the brother, the rudder, is gone. Although the family flounders, it will find a way forward eventually. She realizes she will assume the "sacred privileges and duties" the brother held as caretaker of the aging parents. With foresight, she realizes there will be moments she resents the role thrust on her, but will come to cherish it in time. That so much of a family's past, present, and future could be packed into such a short work is a testament to the writer's talent and mastery of storytelling technique. "Ready About, Hard Alee" represents creative nonfiction at its finest.

— DONNA MEREDITH, Author of *Fraccidental Death*

To Be or Not to Be … a Lawyer

ARIANA KINCAID

I'm not sure I ever really wanted to be a lawyer. I was encouraged to be a lawyer, to be sure. Other professions which appealed to me—nursing, veterinarian, journalist, actress—were discouraged as expensive, unrealistic, or unattainable. Being a lawyer seemed like a reasonable path for someone who had a desire to help people, and whose family had had various and sundry run-ins with the law. My early career following law school revealed my lack of direction beyond obtaining my degree—I worked for state government, clerked for a judge, went back to state government when clerking for a judge left me still eating ramen noodles on a more regular basis than I would have liked. Three years out of law school, I was still making in the $30k range when I saw an ad for a cell tower company which was looking for lawyers to assist with contracts and leasing in West Virginia. I leapt at the opportunity to make fifty grand a year and travel around the state. I also picked up a couple of side gigs—I became an hourly contractor for a law firm which provided pre-paid legal services (a sort of legal insurance, somewhat like medical insurance) statewide, and picked up some acting jobs here and there.

In 2001, a downturn in the economy led to the bankruptcy of the tower company, and I struggled along on the hourly wages at pre-paid legal for a couple of months—during which the country was attacked on September 11. I applied for a job at the Kanawha County Prosecutor's Office, and when asked what I knew about collections of real and personal property taxes, I said, "I don't know, but I'll learn." That honest answer, I was told, landed me the position, and although the salary was not what I was making at the tower company, it was more than I made with the state, and included benefits, unlike the contractual work with pre-paid legal. Two steps forward, one back was perfectly acceptable to me at the age of 30.

Though I was employed by the prosecutor's office, my physical office was in the Kanawha County Sheriff's Department Tax Division. I didn't "belong" in either office—I was the prosecutor who showed up for Christmas and staff meetings at the prosecutor's office, and at the Sheriff's Department, I was a lawyer whose presence was resented by the clerks who thought they were doing a fine job in collections, and who needed me there, anyway? In my off-hours, I immersed myself in community theatre and a job at West Virginia Public Radio.

At some point along the way, I saw an ad for a paying acting job. A program called "Finding Words" was seeking actors to portray children at the end of a week-long conference which trained social workers, police officers, and allied professionals how to interview children who have made disclosures of a sexual nature. We were trained in child development and psychology, as well as some basic legal tenets (which put me a step ahead of the game, understanding "hearsay" and "leading" and other terms of the legal arts) and underwent the same training our future trainees would undergo.

After a couple of years, anticipated administration changes in both offices placed me back in the physical confines of the Prosecutor's office. The office, in an effort to find a job for me to do, essentially re-interviewed me for the job I already had.

The chief deputy prosecutor started with, "Well, we have an opening in the Children's Justice Division. Would that interest you?"

I told him that my parents were social workers, I worked on a clinic project in law school that dealt with juvenile delinquents, I'd been on a grant committee for juvenile justice programs, and I had this new project that I was working with called Finding Words that addressed the needs of abused children. I finished with: "I suppose that will have the flattest learning curve of anything I could be asked to do here."

"Great! Let me introduce you to your new supervisor."

I received about thirty minutes' training in the office of a person who probably thought I wouldn't last long and who may have resented my appointment to her unit, but who gave me the benefit of the doubt anyway. I was able to draw upon her considerable expertise for a few months before a newly elected prosecutor fired her, and separated our unit into the abuse and neglect unit and the juvenile delinquency unit. As the new year began, I and another person landed in a new office with a new supervisor, as the two people assigned to represent Child Protective Services when seeking to remove children from their parents.

In a nutshell, in West Virginia, when a referral is received regarding child abuse and neglect, it is investigated by Child Protective Services. If the allegations contained in the referral are found to have merit, a petition for the removal of the child (or children) from the parents is the next step. My office then defends the Petition in Court against lawyers appointed to represent the parents and children. The convoluted, labyrinthine proceedings can be intimidating to the uninitiated. I was uninitiated.

When I began, I was tentative in court. My cohort had been doing this work a couple of years longer than I had, and she also tried to give me some hints and tips to get me through until I felt more comfortable making decisions and assertions. (Being uncomfortable making these life-altering decisions kept my stress level at an all-time high.) To help prepare myself, I would ask her about some of the lawyers who had been appointed in the cases I filed, so that I could gauge the level of difficulty during a given hearing.

One lawyer, who is now a dear friend, was deemed generally reasonable and willing to work out a compromise during the proceedings. Her client in one instance early on was a repeat offender— she had had a petition filed against her before, and she had gotten her child back. CPS then received another referral, which was investigated, and another petition was filed. I walked off the elevator in front of the courtroom, where my friend and her client were seated.

"What do you want to do today?" I asked, meaning, are we going to have a hearing and put on evidence, or is your client willing to waive her preliminary?

She hissed at me, "What I want is for you to quit picking on my client!"

Alrighty, then.

I did eventually find my footing. It took a horrible case with awful facts and a reluctant witness to make me realize how far I could push to make a point to the court.

CONTENT WARNING: EXTREME CHILD NEGLECT

The social worker came to my office in early February, when I'd been practicing abuse and neglect law for not quite a year. The case as presented resembled only one other case I had experienced at that point, and it was devastating. I was presented photographs of a child who looked to be about three months old, emaciated and with the worst case of diaper rash I'd ever seen. There were several older children in the home. We removed the older children—because, by law, if one child is abused or neglected in a home, it's presumed the other children in the home are, as well. We subpoenaed witnesses. The two parents who resided in the home waived their preliminary hearing; one of the children was placed with their non-offending parent, and the others were placed with a foster family.

Because the mother and father waived their preliminary hearing, we didn't have to call any witnesses to testify. However, those witnesses who had been subpoenaed in case there was a preliminary hearing were subpoenaed again for the adjudication hearing, the next step. Many witnesses understand that the wheels of justice turn slowly, and that sometimes their time is a casualty of the process. Most that rankle over it understand it's for child protections and usually don't complain much.

This one woman, however, was persevering in her attempts to be released from her subpoena. At the time of her first phone call to me, I was unaware of how much she knew about the family and how much she witnessed, if anything. I explained to her that witnesses are very important to the judicial system. I told her that once a subpoena was issued it had the effect of a court order, and that if she didn't appear, the Judge could send a deputy to retrieve her and compel her testimony. She objected. Her mother had a doctor's appointment that she promised her brother she would attend with them. She assured me she knew nothing about the case. She knew only one of the children who attended the school where she volunteered. She insisted she couldn't possibly aid my case.

That hearing was delayed, and I was able to release her from the subpoena. However, a new subpoena was issued, compelling her to testify another day. Again she called. "But I only know the girl. I don't know the other children. I've never met the parents." Again, I explained, "Sometimes what means nothing to you is the point on which the entire case rests." She was unconvinced.

She showed up at the office one day. I went out to meet her. "I thought if I came to your office, I could give a deposition, and I wouldn't have to come to court."

"Well, ma'am, I appreciate the suggestion; however, depositions cannot be conducted at a moment's notice. Opposing counsel would need to be here, their clients would have a right to be here, and there needs to be a court reporter to take it all down. It often takes months to arrange depositions. Not to mention, all of that costs money, and there is simply no budget for depositions in these cases."

She yelled, she implored—I stood firm.

She called again, and this time spoke to my supervisor and complained. I promised I would take her testimony at the next hearing date so that she could put this behind her. Not even that seemed to appease her, but it was the best I could do.

The next date for which she was subpoenaed she appeared, and someone (I can no longer recall who) moved for a continuance. I advised the court that there was a witness present whose testimony was necessary, and who had appeared before when the matter had been continued, and that I'd like to take her testimony that day, and the rest of the matter could be continued. The other parties agreed and the court permitted her testimony. She was sworn in, took the stand, and I established her identity for the court.

Q: Are you a school employee?

A: No.

Q: Are you a volunteer?

A: Yes. I volunteer on my days off at the elementary school where my children attended.

Q: Do some of the children in this case attend that elementary school?

A: Yes. The oldest child, the girl.

Q: Are you acquainted with her through your volunteer work at the school?

A: Yes.

Q: Well acquainted?

A: Yes.

Q: How well?

A: I was sort of assigned to her, or she to me. She needed some extra attention. She missed a lot of school because of various issues, mostly head lice.

Q: Was she truant?

A: Before I got involved, yes.

Q: And after you got involved?

A: I think she made an effort to come to school once I got involved. I was able to give her some extra attention that the teachers and her parents weren't able to give her.

Q: Did you ever pick her up to take her to school?

A: No, but she had lice fairly often, and one time I was asked to take lice treatment items to the family. So I went and got lice shampoo and a comb, and we sat on the front porch and I combed and combed, just nit-picking her hair.

(This was the first time I'd ever heard nit-picking used literally.)

Q: When was this?

A: Early January, when we had that warm snap. We had jackets on, but it wasn't cold.

Q: Was that the only time you visited the home?

She looked at me, silently. I repeated the question.

Q: Was that the only time you visited the home?

She remained silent. The judge ordered her to answer my question.

A: No. I was there again at the end of January.

Q: Why were you there that time?

(I wanted to be able to show a pattern of truancy or chronic lice that could establish neglect, on the off-chance that this incident was not proven as being caused by abuse or neglect.)

A: She wasn't at school, so they asked me to go check on her.

Q: How did that go?

A: Umm … I knocked on the door, and no one answered, so I knocked again and it swung open. I called out to see if anyone was home, but no one answered. I thought I heard something, so I stepped into the house.

Q: What did you find when you got inside?

A: I looked straight down the hallway, and there was someone laying on the bed. I went into the room, and it was the mom and dad, but I couldn't wake them. That's when I heard the noise again, so I looked around some more. When I got to the dining room, I saw a crib by the window.

(At this point, she started crying, and I was happy she was crying.)

Q: Go on.

A: I went over to the crib and there was a doll in it. But then I realized that the noise I heard was a baby crying.

(She began to cry harder.)

A: And what I thought was a doll was a baby.

(There were more tears. The bailiff handed her a tissue. Her sobs and the ticking of the clock were the only sounds in the courtroom.)
Q: Then what happened?
She sobbed again, and sighed.
A: I covered him up with a blanket, and I left.

The child was dead within a matter of days of her visit. She was likely the last person outside the child's family to see him alive. She never wanted her own feelings of guilt to see the interior of a courtroom. The incident haunts me and his autopsy photos remain in my mind.

Stepping outside of my comfort zone—forcing her hand—lit a fire in me that illuminated my path, leading me to become a better lawyer, and a better advocate for children.

||||||||||||||||||||||||||||||||||||||||||||||||||||||||||||||||||||||||||||||||||||||||||||||||||||||||||||||||||||||||||||||||||||||||||||||||||||||||||||||||||||||||||||||||||||||||||||||||||||||

Ms. Kincaid's winding path, a combination of pursuing goals that seemed "reasonable" and saying "Yes!" to interesting new opportunities, led her to a career as a lawyer. The legal profession is dominated by procedure and scheduling: if you aren't sure what's next, follow procedure, schedule the next step, and eventually your case will reach some sort of end. As her legal career progressed she was, at times, uncertain, but she followed procedure; she scheduled next steps.

One reluctant witness, a scheduling problem, changed everything. In the midst of a heartbreaking case, at a defining moment, Ms. Kincaid followed her gut, stood up, pushed, didn't take no for an answer. It changed everything.

Ms. Kincaid writes with clarity and just a hint of self-effacing humor. I was honored to be along for the journey.

— CYNTHIA TOOMEY, MFA, legal professional,
reluctant writer, cello owner, cat lover

Suite of Five Poems

KARI GUNTER-SEYMOUR

||||||||||||||||||||||||||||||||||||||||||||||||||||||||||||||||||||||||||||||||||||

ALL SHE COULD ABIDE

Because her job was to stay clean and thankful,
mostly invisible, as though telling her what to do
told her who she was, she rubbed basil

between finger and thumb to breathe the inside
of a thing, walked the verges of muddy stream,
sugared scarp and hilly breast, clear

of knotted root and dirt-wrapped wire,
color-flushed on wildflowers, her mind a buzz
of song, psalm and sonnet.

Here. A dead bird. A tiny Christ, riven
in light. Her sorrow lifted in wisps and moans
to the mouth of the wind.

In some languages *to be carried*
is the same as *to fly*.

Shedding blouse, skirt, tender garments,
she opens her flesh to pain-ripened sun,
sways to the pitch and pluck of sky.

MY FRIEND LORAINE ASKS WILL I GO WITH HER TO A DRAG SHOW

Loraine, heart of a star, rainwater-rusted,
walks with strange steps in jumpy rhythms
from the mountains. She once made
a cardboard cutout of a cloud and that cloud's
sister, sent to me as a postcard.

I pray most nights standing,
worry about the wind when it presses
hard from the south, walk
beneath lightning to gather up chickens.

That night the bourbon tasted like Koolaid.
We drank five each, together a twisted mirror
of becoming better selves.
During the finale, we hiked up our skirts,
cavorted like dervishes.

A rainbow of zinnias swayed the sidewalk,
moonlit, as Loraine and I tittered homeward,
holding fast to one another, spouting new found
revelations of womanness, noting that serious
dancing might be the cure for years of heavy lifting.

She reminds me how a seed case splits,
exposes backbone but also vulnerability.
Shit fire, Loraine says, *we should*
all throw ourselves like seed.

BADASSES

Sunday afternoon. Taylor Swift's latest nonsense
caterwauls the radio, a third-string agitation,
compared to my son trying to bootlick his daughter
into jumping in our pond off the high dive,
nine feet up a steep planked ladder.

A pinch of a girl, she just this week turned six
and I wonder where that rascal in him comes from.
I blame his father, long gone and good riddance.
My true husband, a gem, who knows me all too well,
taps his sandaled foot against my pinky-toe,
slightly shakes his head, because my granddaughter
just cold-shouldered her daddy, ran to fetch
her fishing pole instead.

Though I don't want it, those twelve soccer boys,
clear the other side of the world, are on my mind.
Trapped miles inside a cave, tides rising, huddled
and hungry, licking water drops from crusty walls.
Last week, Navy SEALs rose from the depths
like apparitions, brought pep talks, promises,
concocting on the fly, ways those boys, who don't
even know how to swim, can strap on a face mask,
practice a few strokes, MacGyver their way free.

We cool ourselves in the water, ride four-wheelers,
reach for icy Coca-Colas, popsicles, slices of melon.
We're fixing to wind down when breaking
news grabs the radio. *Christ almighty*,
four of those boys made it out, others

not far behind, SEALs at their backs, urging.

Soon after, my wily son afloat below the dive,
that plucky grandbaby of mine sets down her pole,
climbs the ladder, leaps like a fish-nymph,
hoots as she breaks the surface.

WOMEN'S MARCH
WASHINGTON, BY GOD, D.C.

Down the mountains, out the hollers
they troop, muck boots and flannel.
Plans made firm at the women's
auxiliary meetings, passed booth-to-booth
at the farmer's market.

Their husbands' mouths gaped,
they board the bus, middle of the night,
cardboard signs and children in tow,
their bodies a poem of spine
and gut and cicada music.
Some have never before left the county.

On the morning of the event,
Rita Rae Widener counts her egg money,
jogs from hen house to barn.
Her litter of piglets nearly ready for market,
will bring a good price.
Next time, no matter what Delbert says,
she's going to be on that bus.

DAUGHTER-IN-LAW MINE, ONCE REMOVED

there is a wall on the US/Mexico border
made of surplus steel and wire mesh.
A thousand miles worth, back yards
and alleys in Chula Vista, as *far* up as Temecula.
Children stand on our side, poke tiny fingers
against those *hardly even holes* for the slightest
brush of their grandmother's fingers,
pressed inward from the Tijuana side
I saw it in *Time* magazine and cried, my own fingers
urgent, the iciness of your Colorado stand-off,
rigid as anything man-made.

Surely you remember this rich Ohio soil,
ripe to bursting, water pure, pastures plush.
A woman can make her way here.
I don't care about the details, who was right,
who should have got what, but didn't.
I don't mind that you will never love again,
and hell's to pay.

I care my body has gone to wrinkle
and the world to concrete and convenience.
Tractors traded for fracking augers,
though this parcel will never fall,
long as I can steady a shotgun.
With no partner but a wall to cling to,
what's balled up can only bounce back.
Raised without old ways, a granddaughter
might never make out why
her body aches for seed and trowel.

It came to me, riffling *National Geo*,
to send this telescope, highly
recommended for its ability to reflect.
Along with the moon and stars,
help her *please* to look south of Lake Erie,
by way of the Appalachians, then east-by-southeast.
Tell her that's her grandmother,
top of Beck's Knob, waving a white hankie.

―――――――――――――――――――――――――――――――――

"In some languages to be carried/is the same as to fly," writes Kari Gunter-Seymour.
In these poems she carries us along on a current of words, again and again, as we
see the woman in the poems take off, pull free, throw herself head first into life's
Sturm und Drang. No longer content to be carried, this voice aims to take flight.

— **RITA QUILLEN**, Author of *Wayland*

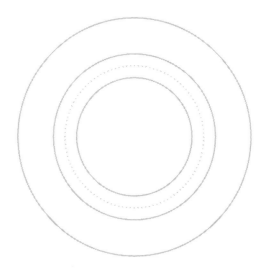

Inheritance

LYDIA A. CYRUS

There is something about the way the trees lean. They arch across
the paved road toward the house, our house. At the darkest points
of the night they glow—white, naked trees that reach far above me
and deep below. It is not the trees themselves that stand out. It's the
darkness that fills every space between them. Every gap of space
between the branches is full of the night. I stand before them and
look ahead, staring straight into the middle of the trees. Something is
there, something old that lived long before I did. It is not immediately
noticeable and does not stir. I am accustomed to it and therefore I am
aware of what it looks, sounds, and feels like. Suddenly a warm gust of
late April air arrives and wraps my face in an embrace. It smells clean,
like water, and my hair becomes unfurled. *There is something in the trees.*
There was always something in the trees.

The heartache is on me. My mother is sitting in the passenger
seat of my car. The air conditioning in my black car was working hard,
overtime. Combating the heat of a Saturday evening in May. My hair
was shorter, longer depending on who you asked, but still dark and
thick enough that I felt the heat radiating off my temples and into
my roots. There are two distinct fingerprints on the windshield, just
above the steering wheel. My index and middle fingers, left behind
from a morning in late February when a sheet of ice covered the glass.
I touched it. Wondering exactly how cold it could be, how cold it was.
The grooves of my skin are still there.

Driving down the road I feel myself being pulled backward. Up
and down the hill, not over, where we just came from back to the plot
of land where my aunt lived. In reality, I was driving a hot car. Going
twenty-five on a bumpy road but in my mind I was standing in the

gravel driveway that used to lead to her home. It leads to nothing now. Her house is gone, nothing is left. It has been one year and six months since she died and even now grief fills every pore. The sweat beaded on my neck mixes with the abrasive chill of the air pumping through the vents. She never saw my black car. She never saw a lot of things.

The story, when we were children, was that a demon lived in her house. A black, shadow man that remained in the spare bedroom on the left side of the house. Several of the younger cousins in the family saw him and almost no one, besides our Aunt, would sleep in that house. That was the story then.

The story now is that I want to build a house there. On the light brown surface where her house stood. The plot of land that for everything about it, minus its invisibility, looks like home. The butterfly bushes still rooted in the same places and the pebbles from the garden still tossed in the same piles. If I close my eyes and point, I can still find the back door, the bathroom with the skylight, the bedroom, the kitchen. Her life—the memories of it—are what keep the house built even after its destruction. The gravel driveway has only just started to grow over.

My mother wonders if the demon would come to live in my house too. I would hate to tell her that I've already thought about that. Already cast the scene in my mind of what it would feel and look like if I found a shadow man in the spare bedroom. I had already decided that the spirit of my Aunt, in her spark, would tell him to leave. Instead of shadows, I imagined that it would smell like flowers. Outside, there would be birds nesting in the crooks and angles of the porch. All of the things that were there when she was. Including the shape of her.

When they tore down the house my Aunt grew up in, they pulled out a Ouija board. Two of them. The very first ones that Hasbro—yes, Hasbro—had ever created. No one could recall who they had belonged to. *It must have been your great grandmother's.* The great grandmother who died in 1987. The boards went home with other relatives, who, in a fever dream of intoxication, decided to use them. The last word I had ever heard of the matter was that one of the boards had been cut up and buried. The ritual, according to popular belief, of proper disposal of a Ouija board.

My Aunt was not a witch or even a believer in magic so far as I can guess. She made no comments about the boards when they were found. Nothing again when they were cut and buried. Our connection to each other feels so strong that I have often wondered if she isn't hoping I'll pick up a board. Perhaps one from a used bookstore that sits on the shelf labeled OCCULT. But then again, she must still know, as she always had before, that I would never touch one. If she wants to tell me something, she'll have to return in another way. Sometimes she does return, in dreams. It isn't clear that it's her all of the time. But sometimes, in the shape of a lioness, she is there.

When I lived in West Virginia, she looked like herself. Before she fell sick. She would talk and I would listen. I would wake and cry uncontrollably and suffer through the waking hours as though I had never slept at all. I wanted to see her but not at a cost. I could only afford so much, so little.

I am what the poets call *a permeable person*. Permeable as in allowing liquids or gasses to pass through. By another poet's definition, I am a lightning rod prone to being struck by the emotions of others. I am willed to believe that I am one of many and I am one from a long line of other women, like my Aunt, who were seers. Maybe I believed this only a little when I lived in West Virginia, my homeland. Maybe it was like a whisper I had in church or on the school bus once or twice.

I really believed it though when I moved away and she became a lion.

She first became a lion one night when I dreamed about her house. Some of us were gathered there and outside we heard screaming. This is a different kind of lion, a faux lion. The mountain variety, which science claims is long dead and extinct in our slice of the world. To scare them, you must stand tall and scream back. As I did in the dream. You scream until your voice is blood and your eyes water. Your nose, thinking that you have fallen ill, might run too. Your skin becomes red and still you scream because, if not, you will die.

Around the edges of the bushes and the trees came the lions to her house. But once they rushed closer, I could see that they were African lions. Females. I retreated from the screaming and the standing and tried to slide the glass door shut between us. As I did so, the big female licked my hand. I shut the door and found myself deep within my Aunt's house. The same it always had been but now there were lions. Lions with rough, feline tongues.

The dream dictionary says that a lioness in your dreams spells maternal instinct. When they attack, it suggests that someone is invading your family bond. My Aunt was testing me. Reminding me that I have within me, already, instinct that I cannot lose. Lest I fall apart and vanish.

My Aunt is desperate to reach me. Because she died when I had just turned twenty-one and things are serious now. I've left our homeland for the Midwest and as I have crossed many rivers and bodies of water to get there, her image has had a harder time passing through. She must have decided on the image of lions because she knows I am feline myself. In all the years previous to this one, I was a bear humble and unseen. But once I moved away, I became more on edge, not sleeping or hibernating. I became a tiger.

But then, back home, there is an infestation of lions. The mountain variety. At home, in the hollow we live in, there is one. Maybe two. The tracks have been found and the screaming can be heard there. When I visit, I'm told about it but I never see it. I'm warned about it. Told not to walk alone at night and to watch my surroundings. This is what the people from outside of here do not know: It comes from the trees or a ledge. Someplace high. Undetected. Then it leaps. Then it kills. This is the way things have been done for hundreds of years. This is the way of the lion.

My Aunt died the week before Christmas. This year, the two-year anniversary, she made sure to pay a visit. Since I have moved, I have not seen her as a woman. This is how I know that she's serious now, because she has become a predator. I went to bed, draped underneath her old afghans, sleeping in her bed which I had inherited. In the middle of the night, I dreamed that I was standing on the bridge that crosses into our driveway. In the yard, there was a deer. A large one, but its antlers, if there were any, were obscured. Then there was screaming.

The lion pounced from behind, from a small tree which has been growing on the creek bank for years. It latched into the sides of the deer and bit down on the neck. There was thrashing, moaning, cries from both parties. When the deer was dead, the lion stood there and looked at me. I woke up, terribly afraid that I had sleepwalked into something I could not wake from.

According to the dream dictionary, deer represent grace and all of the traits that, when found in a woman, are good. To dream that you are hunting or killing a deer means that you are suppressing feminine qualities.

My Aunt wants me to know how to kill naivety. Innocence. Foolishness. She wants me to know that I have to seize the vulnerable parts of myself and kill them. From the trees, from behind in silence, in a leap and bound. Our connection is still strong. She and I are both alive and we are both feline.

But this is just a story. Someday when I'm older it might be told differently.

||||||||||||||||||||||||||||||||||||||||||||||||||||||||||||||||||||||||||||||||||||||||||||||||||||||||||||||||||||||||||||||||||||||||||||||||||||||||||||||||||||||||||||||||||||

The word inheritance does not always mean the acquisition of material objects from a loved one's passing. It can have a visceral component, a bestowal of a legacy shared with that person. A gift unique to both and a bounding of souls that even death cannot break.

— LINDA RIFFE, Retired Librarian

Ruminations of a Coal Miner's Ex-wife

KANDI WORKMAN

|||||||||||||||||||||||||||||||||||||||||||||||||||||||||||||||||||||

Tonight I watched *Blood on the Mountain* for the first time.

I'm a West Virginia UMWA coal miner's daughter. Granddaughter of coal miners and coal miners' wives. Both of my parents came from coal camps in Mingo County, and my granny's camphouse in Ragland was adjoined to an old mining bathhouse that my papaw converted to a workshop. My dad said his great, great uncle used to own all the land down the left fork of Pigeon Creek, from Delbarton on. Said taxes ate him alive and a coal company bought almost all his land, except Curry Hollow near the foot of Cow Creek Mountain, if memory served him rightly.

When I was growing up, I swore to the moon and stars I'd never be a coal miner's wife, no way, no how. Strikes. Layoffs. All that dust and dirty buckets and heavy boots. The scares. Dad was covered in 22 Holden in 1997, when I was 18. A version of him survived.

I married when I was 19. A buggy boy at Black's Foodland turned factory worker in Nitro turned water pipeliner doing a federal job in Cabin Creek turned coal miner by the time he was 22. The money called to him, and like a receptive lover he went. He just couldn't say no. I became a coal miner's wife, and neither of us was ever the same.

Jeremy eventually went to work at Revolution, the Massey mine in Boone County, WV, near where we both grew up. He was a Massey "member," terminology pointed out in *Blood on the Mountain* that was used to create a false sense of place in a serf-like system. My family went to the Massey clinic on Main Street in Madison, a medical facility established by Massey, and our visits were paid with Massey money.

We attended Massey Day in Logan several times (all hail Massey). We even played with "Massey bucks," an incentive program in which employees could accrue points based on attendance and safety to purchase items from the Massey catalog. Anything from clothing to guns to toys to vacations, it was in there. We even owned the Masseyopoly board game (a gift from the company). That's not a joke.

Money was better than good. Jeremy took classes for a year and a half while he worked and completed an apprenticeship to receive his underground electrician cards. A decade later, by the time we separated, he could bring home $8k a month during a time-intensive, soul-sucking work month, seven days a week at 12 hours or more, usually when it was time to pull out and move the long wall. There's nothing that makes less sense than using exhausted, work-torn men to do one of the most dangerous tasks underground. Revolution was not family-friendly, but he couldn't say no.

I admit I'm still heavy with guilt when I think of the end of my marriage and the demise of the traditional Appalachian family Jeremy and I had created. It wasn't my fault. It wasn't his. I know this now. However, in the beginning of the end, from admittance to acceptance, I blamed him, inwardly, as I performed the "it's not you, it's me" bit. He was an insecure man, I thought, and I knew hearing his wife say she wanted to end a 13-year marriage wasn't going to forge his self-worth. I wanted to verbally own all the blame and guilt, gladly and willingly, if it meant I could get out of the dark hole I lived in day after day.

I didn't understand it then, didn't understand why he couldn't say no, why I was raising my kids on my own, why I had become his maid and cook and personal shopper, among other things, except his friend. Why did he want so badly for me to become friends with his mining buddies' wives? Ugh. Like, you're in a hole with these guys more than you're with your family, and then you want to spend all your free time with them (he couldn't say no), and choose their wives as my friends because I have no freedom to go out and make my own? An almost inescapable numbness settled in.

Tonight I watched *Blood on the Mountain*.

Jim messaged the other day to tell me Merry Christmas. He was Jeremy's section boss when we split. He and Jeremy used to ride together, third shift, so he'd be at the house every evening and every morning. When Jeremy'd get to talking hateful, Jim'd look at him and say, "Now, Pup, you shouldn't talk to your ole lady that way. She's a mighty gracious, lovely woman, and if my wife did half as much as she does for you, I'd be pampering her every day and she'd never have to take out the trash." Jeremy's response: "She's the toughest woman I know. Stronger than any man. She can handle it." But I couldn't.

Jim's mom died the other day, and it makes me wonder what his thoughts about life are now.

I watched *Blood on the Mountain*.

I watched my life play out before me, the parts I understood and remembered, parts familiar and friendly, and the revelations of things known but not seen. Living here in Southern WV is very much like not being able to see the forest for the trees. So much of what went wrong in my marriage went wrong because my then-husband was being exploited and made to think that he had the good life. No—he was made to think he had the best life. He couldn't say no.

One Sunday morning, mid-Dec in 2010, I woke up, went downstairs, and sat at the kitchen table. The house was still, dark. I was so much in my head, mood-flat, teeter-tottering with suicidal flashes of images that I would wish away immediately. It was like that table was a pillar and around me, where there was supposed to be support, there was nothing. I thought, yet again, "Is this the life I'm going to live until I die?" Jeremy came down, smiling, all the kids still in bed. Maybe I was crying. Not sobbing-crying, with sound and theatrics, but the kind of cry when tears melt from the slits of your eyes with no emotion attached to them because the emotion is tucked 300 feet deep somewhere inside, and the tears flow from that swollen well without effort. He asked what was wrong. Calmly, without a shift in emotion, I told him our marriage, our life, was wrong, and I wanted a divorce. With a spark of joy, I became elated and smiled because I had spoken that truth to life. I laughed. I laughed in the midst of his pain and humiliation and fear and immediate sense of abandonment. I laughed the laugh of recognition.

His words to me were, "But, our life is perfect."

I had to say no.

[Blood on the Mountain (2016) is a documentary that encapsulates historical and contemporary issues stemming from the coal mining industry in Central Appalachia, including corporate greed, a corrupt political system, exploitation of the mountains and its people, and the folks who stood and still stand together in solidarity to fight big money power and the government. (Directed by Mari-Lynn Evans and Jordan Freeman, Evening Star Productions)]

Reading "Ruminations of a Coal Miner's Ex-Wife" is a bit like following Kandi Workman into the mine of her own heart. She leads you through the weight and darkness of generations of her family who had been swallowed by the coal mines. Then she takes you into her own lightless experiences all while expertly pointing out the vein of love that drew her in for so long.

— JOSIE DORANS, Author of From Fingers of Bone

Self-Portrait As Arboreal Being

MEG MATICH

Do not, darkling.
I have done enough, spun years
The heft of cobwebs.
Lice poisoned my careful limbs.
I transpired
In gasps under the massif weight

Mouth stuffed
With moss blooms.
Blame me: I am
The pristine memories
I did not have before.

I have forgotten everything except—
You did this.
—ionally.
But have me.
I have never been haven to anyone.

For those / of us / whose witness / is born / where swords / become cups / as cups / become swords.

— RANDI WARD, Author, *Whipstitches*

Gargoyles

DEBBIE HAGAN

||||||||||||||||||||||||||||||||||||||||||||||||||||||||

In 1990, I sat at a linen-draped table in one of Manhattan's midtown Chinese restaurants waiting for my old boss from St. Louis to walk through the door. In a city filled with great restaurants, he had to pick the one that had a funeral parlor ambiance: blood red velvet décor, strange Muzak buzzing from tinny speakers, and an odd pickle smell.

Hours earlier, I had been in my office, proofreading a two-page ad going into Sunday's *New York Times*, when he called. I knew it was Bill by the long, flat Midwestern vowels. I'd worked five years for him before getting married, moving to New Jersey, and becoming marketing director for an international publisher. It'd been a year since I'd seen him.

He prattled on and on about clients and co-workers we both knew, while I stared out the window watching the sun paint a rose gold over the Chrysler Building and etch deep shadows into its steel eagle gargoyles. I remembered how photographer Margaret Bourke-White used to keep a studio near the gargoyles on the sixty-fourth floor.

During the building's construction, welders and riveters told her, "When you are working at 800 feet above ground, make believe that you are at eight feet and relax." They coaxed her to onto one of the gargoyle's steely beaks. There she dangled with her big box camera in the air taking some of the city's most iconic photographs.

"Look, I'm only in town today, so why don't we grab lunch—my treat," my old boss said.

"I have an ad to finish up."

"Come on," he insisted. "Everyone has to eat."

The old salesman's strategy: beg until she says yes.

As I waited in the restaurant, I couldn't help but think, I was no longer Bill's *girl*. All of us on the magazine—newbie or seasoned journalist, twenty-five or forty-five—we had all been *girls*. We interviewed artists and art dealers around the country, attended glitzy parties, stayed in swanky hotels, and occasionally met celebrities. It felt glamorous, and the bosses figured this into our meager pay.

At an awards banquet in Chicago, Bill introduced each *girl* to the audience. As he announced our names, we stood. He gave our title and then an odd and embarrassing personal quip. When he came to me, he laughed and said, "Well, this is our *blonde* editor." The crowd laughed and that was it. No name, no title.

It turned into a running joke: *Here comes the blonde editor.* I didn't take it personally. Bill was a kindly old guy—albeit, a bit of a goof. He'd taken a chance on me and nurtured my career. I appreciated it.

Eventually, I began taking a harder look at the publishing company that produced our magazine. It had three tiers: salesmen in suits; *girl*s writing, photographing, editing, and producing the magazines; and a handful of faceless support staff. Our magazine was like a catalog—400-plus pages every month, half being ads. The suits—guys selling the ads—benefited the most. The *girls* traveled, often staying in four-star hotels, treating themselves, and a client or two, to lobster dinners and a Broadway play. The suits figured as long as the girls remained happy and didn't beg for big raises, they'd overlook these little indulgences.

In the restaurant, I noticed Bill trotting down the street, his Burberry raincoat tails flying, his battered leather briefcase swinging, his umbrella waving above his head. In the foyer, he shook like an old hound dog, dropping his gear, placing his hat on a hook.

I raised my hand, wiggled my fingers. His eyes lit up. Before he walked toward me, he placed his left arm under his right elbow. His right hand pivoted, slapping his cheek, triggering a big eye roll.

His Jack Benny routine. Oh, I'd forgotten all about this.

He stood frozen, displaying this wretched "woe-is-me" expression. I laughed, which seemed the only thing to do. Yet, I hated myself.

Bill sauntered to my table, then scooted his chair close to mine. He leaned over and whispered into my hair, "I've missed you so much." His breath misted my cheek.

Then, I felt something like a spider creeping up my nylons … but it was bigger and far more menacing. I flicked it away. I knew I should say something, but my conscience begged, *Let it go. If it weren't for him, you wouldn't be here. You wouldn't even have this job. You owe him this.*

It triggered a memory, back six years when Bill hired me. I'd interviewed with him twice. Each time he'd read my resume, asked ridiculous questions, then thumbed through my writing and photography samples. He complimented my work, but didn't offer a job.

The third time, he finally asked, "So, why four employers in six years?"

I'd practiced my response: "I've been building up my writing and photography skills, preparing for a job like this."

He studied me as if I'd made this up.

I could have explained how I'd come from a long line of tradesmen, housewives, farmers, and factory workers. No one in my family had gone to college. In fact, Mom had only an eighth grade education, Dad maybe a sixth. I turned to TV for role models, and there found Ann Marie, a character (played by Marlo Thomas) in the late 60s show *That Girl*. She had everything I ever wanted: her own apartment in New York City, stylish clothes, glamorous jobs. She struggled sometimes, but always bounced back, determined to reach her goal: being a Broadway actress.

After college, I became a reporter on my hometown newspaper. Apparently, no woman had ventured into the reporters' corner in a long time. Papers and photographs were piled high on desks, and a thick cloud of cigarette smoke, greasy take-out food, and stale beer hung in the air. Male reporters eyed me over their reading glasses. I found my desk, my broken-down typewriter, and a chair and sat down to work.

Wednesdays were always late nights writing last-minute stories, making final edits, and proofing. Pizza, beer, whiskey, and weed fueled these evenings. I felt out of place. I was barely twenty-one, raised a

Southern Baptist, and worried that the police would come and arrest us all or I'd be fired and unable to find another job. So, I remained straight, avoiding the editor who grew ever louder and more animated. He'd repeatedly asked for a blowjob in the darkroom. My face flamed. I couldn't even look at him. Eventually, he grabbed my arms, dragged me caveman style, while shouting to our co-workers, "Now we'll see what develops!"

They laughed.

I scurried away like a little mouse, embarrassed, and believing that I must have done something to cause this. I thought back to my girlhood idol, Ann Marie. If a man ever spoke rudely to her or made a pass, she'd become indignant, tell him to stop, and he would do just that.

I found another job. Then another. Each time, I hoped for kinder male colleagues and more female co-workers. However, in Missouri in the late 1970s, few women held professional jobs, other than teachers, secretaries, nurses, and bookkeepers.

For a while, I worked and lived at a lake resort, where I produced a small, local magazine. One day my boss asked for photographs of new property being developed. One of the guys with whom I'd joked around in the mornings around the coffeepot offered to drive me there in his boat. Once we'd traveled beyond land sight, he grabbed me, pinned me to the floor, yanked off my clothes, ignoring my pleas for him to stop. At the very last second, he gave up and acted shocked when I threatened to report him to the company's director. His eyes grew wide and he shouted, "For God's sake, don't tell anyone. I have a wife, kids, a mortgage. No one needs to know about this. Nothing happened. *Nothing.*"

Well, nothing happened to him. I was bruised and shaken, unable to go back to my office. I couldn't talk to anyone about this—not even my fiancé. He'd demand I go to the police ... or at least report it to my boss. Trouble was, this guy was the company's number one salesman. I'd be fired. Not him. I'd seen this before.

Again, I wondered, had I done something to cause this? Had I misled this guy by simply being friendly, joking around so casually?

Did this make me easy or a pushover or a girl who didn't know how to say no, who would just go with the flow and have sex with whomever, whenever and never tell? This deeply troubled me.

Certainly, I hadn't lied telling Bill during our interview that I was building up my writing and photography skills for a magazine job like his. That was true, but I'd also left jobs feeling physically threatened and in emotional distress, but I didn't want to discuss it.

In any case, Bill offered me the job. He walked around his desk, threw his arms around me, and pulled me into a big bear hug. My eyes darted to the assistant publisher, who groaned, then looked away.

In the Chinese restaurant, Bill snapped his fingers at the waiter, who ignored him. When he passed back by, Bill yelled, "Hey, bring us a bottle of champagne."

I sighed. "Bill. I have work to do this afternoon."

He stuck out his bottom lip, rolled his eyes, and made this God-awful pouty face.

The champagne arrived in a shiny silver stand. Bill threw back one glass, then another, all the while telling me about his sailboat, new BMW, and his profit-sharing money, which had made him practically a millionaire.

When I'd left the company, I had earned just enough profit-sharing money for a small home down payment.

I pushed sweet and sour pork around my plate, plotting my exit. I was no longer Bill's *girl*...nor anyone's *girl*. I wasn't Ann Marie, either. I was just me, a woman lucky enough to land a great job in New York City. I was still finding my way, learning the ropes, navigating the complexities of this city and this job, and I certainly didn't need Bill or anyone else erecting unnecessary roadblocks.

I remembered the joy I felt arriving for work that first day in Manhattan, rising out of the subway and stepping onto Third Avenue. It was like being in the center of a giant heartbeat—the blur of traffic, pound of feet, cries for taxis, blares of horns. The island throbbed, vibrating every cell in me.

I loved this city, but had so much to learn. I tried ordering a ham sandwich at a Jewish deli. I'd become lost for hours in Brooklyn. When I failed to obtain black market tickets to a sold-out performance of *Les Misérables* for our Japanese clients, my boss threw such a tantrum, I thought he'd fire me on the spot. At night, I'd lie awake, reliving my mistakes, ranting over stupid choices. But I was determined. I would make it.

I'd become friendly with our company's owner and CEO. At first, I'd see him in the foyer, at the end of the day, and we'd exchanged glances.

One night, he strode over to me and asked, "You know who you look like?"

I cringed. It was always someone with a big mouth, overbite, and mountainous cheekbones: Carol Burnett, Joni Mitchell, or Carol Channing.

"Leslie Caron," he said.

I'd never heard that one, but I liked it—someone beautiful and French.

"You know, I'm going to call you Gigi," he said, then he smiled and walked away.

Looking at pictures of Leslie Caron, I didn't see the resemblance. However, over time, I realized it wasn't so much a physical resemblance he saw, but something within me—my girlish energy, eagerness to please, desperate need to succeed.

One day he called me into his office saying he wanted to discuss the new ad agency I was hiring. I was puzzled. We'd already made this decision. When I showed up in his office, he spoke softly, gently, "Gigi, you're a beautiful young lady, but you've got to hold your head up. You need to look clients in the eye. Be proud of who you are."

I didn't know what to say. No one had ever spoken to me like this, not my parents, not my teachers, not my friends, not even my husband.

I saw an image of myself walking around New York City with my head down, eyes cast away, face filled with fear. Was this me?

Sometimes I did feel like an injured animal—cowering, slumping into myself, suffering in silence. But I'd been doing this a long time.

I studied the women on the streets, the way they took long, quick strides, tucking their purses under their arms like footballs, keeping their faces fierce, determined, suspicious of everyone. I listened to the way they talked in meetings, speaking insistently, staring clients down. No one—not even the men—would mess with them. In contrast, I was Gigi—a crème puff—sweet, fragile and easy to chew. No more.

Once my former boss had finished his lunch and the entire bottle of champagne, he reached over and grabbed my hand. I tried to pull it back, but he held on.

Then, he looked at me and said, "I'm … well … I'm in love with you."

At first, I thought he'd said *I love you*. That I could understand, because I'd felt deeply for co-workers who'd worked hard, persisted against adversity, and acted generously, sometimes making me look better than I really was.

But when I looked into my old boss's gray eyes, I knew what he'd said, *I'm in love with you*. That implied a certain intimacy that never existed—something you say to your wife, your lover, or the woman you'd like to take to your hotel room.

Gigi might have blushed, laughed it off, and turned it into a joke: *For God sakes, Bill. The champagne's gone to your head.*

I did not.

I stood up, looked down at my old boss, the man who'd given my career a boost, but who looked gray, withered, and a bit sheepish. I don't remember saying anything but *I've got to go*. I didn't want to make a scene, yet I wanted him to know, I was not that girl.

Then the irony of our situation struck me. I was now one of the major advertisers in his magazine. I did not need him. My company probably didn't need him either. In fact, it was up to me whether we continued to advertise with him or not.

I marched onto 42nd Street, pausing at Lexington, looking up at the Chrysler Building, its pointed chromium-nickel steel arches rising like a crown. They gleamed in the noon sun, and my spirits soared.

I thought of Margaret Bourke-White crawling out onto one of those gargoyles. She understood just what the welders had said: *eight or eight hundred feet, it's all the same thing.*

Now I understood too. It's all about holding your head up, finding your balance, and refusing to fall.

The photographer Margaret Bourke-White hung on a gargoyle during the construction of the Chrysler building in New York City and made iconic photographs. Like her, Debbie Hagan writes a memorable story of a journey from being "one of the girls" to becoming a woman who finds her independence and balance. This narrative of a journey, rich with sensory details, is one that all women can relate to.

— LEILA RYLAND SWAIN, Jungian psychologist and writer

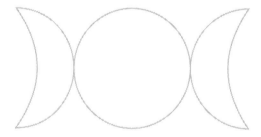

Star Child

CAT PLESKA

||||||||||||||||||||||||||||||||||||||||

Maria believed in aliens and ghosts. She said to me once: "You are a Star Child." How could I not be drawn to someone who told me this? At the time I didn't know what a Star Child was, but it sounded magic.

When Maria was four, she and her twin sister, born to a poor family, were put in an orphanage in her rural state. It was not uncommon in the early to mid 20th century. At least, they would be housed, fed, clothed. The intent was to retrieve them when their family could afford them.

In Maria's and her sister's case, her grandfather interceded. He plucked them from the orphanage and sold them for $200 each to a couple from Ohio. How this became a legal adoption, Maria didn't know, nor ever learned the details. To her, what reverberated through her soul was that she was sold.

Maria and I met in the late 80s through a club of women spouses that gathered monthly. All of our husbands were working at the same plant in the south. The club was called Stitch and Bitch—mostly no stitching but plenty of good-natured bitching. And eating. We tried a different restaurant each month.

I felt myself gravitate toward Maria, with her warm smile, huge brown eyes, her throaty laugh. She was seven years my senior, but with her slim figure, milky skin, and coiffed reddish brown hair she looked much younger. We often talked by phone and visited one another in between Stitch and Bitch meetings. We shopped together and drank gallons of coffee and talked non-stop. Eventually, Maria began to reveal some of her past to me.

Her first marriage, at a young age, resulted in her three children. The marriage ended because they both cheated. It was a wild, tempestuous relationship, with much passion and not much maturity. They realized they were too young, the children came too quickly, and it was best to move on.

A second marriage followed to a member of a famous boxer's fight camp, a sparring boxer who didn't hesitate to try out pugilistic moves on Maria. Once he bodily threw her over the coffee table. She knew nothing would change, so she eventually took her children and left. I never learned how she survived with her children when she had to make it on her own. She was silent about those in between times. I don't know if she was being secretive or just wanted to put parts of her life behind her.

By the time we met, two of her children were grown and out of the house, leaving only a sixteen-year-old son at home. He started to go off the rails a bit, she told me, so she put him in a one-day program called Scared Straight. Young teens, teetering on mischief, perhaps crime, got to see just how bad it can be in jail and the process the police and courts put you through. He apparently was impressed enough to finish high school relatively unscathed. I wasn't sure I could have done that had it been my daughter swaying to the wrong side of right.

When we all arrived in the same town, Maria had married her third husband only a year before, and they appeared happy. She mentioned to me one day, however, early on in our friendship, that he was secretive, but ironically she offered no details.

Over the next year and a half, Maria revealed her thinking about the paranormal, aliens, ghosts and what she believed was various humans' ability to heal. I was in my mid-thirties and just beginning to study non mainstream beliefs, such as Native American tribal religions, all popular subject matter in America then. But I was not as deeply involved in any studies as she was. She believed in human transformation to a happier time on earth; she imagined all whom she loved in the white light of healing and protection. As we grew closer, she told me the remainder of the story of when she was sold. Her adoptive father molested her and her identical twin sister. I felt sickened at the thought, but I managed to ask if her mother knew at the time the abuse was happening. She said she suspected that her mother did but had done or said nothing. I thought that such a reality must have sent Maria on a quest for something to anchor her, to believe in.

When she and her sister were young women, they founded a paranormal society. This is where their curiosity began for other realities, as she had experienced it. She knew spirits hovered around all of us. "You can know they are there, hear them, even see them sometimes, if you're open to the idea," she said. I told her of my paranormal experiences when I was a child, and she nodded. "Yes, of course you would have seen objects moving, heard voices." That's when she turned to me and said, "You are a Star Child."

"What?" I was puzzled. I'd been reading some of the books she'd loaned me about her metaphysical interests, but this was a new concept to me. She explained: "There's a theory that some people were seeded in the stars and then put on this earth to behave in particular ways."

I was fascinated but I had questions: What are these 'ways'? Who put us here? At this point, I wasn't skeptical as much as curious. I'd gone this far in my studies with her, and I had grown to trust that *she* believed in these unusual ideas.

She rose to go to her bookshelf. She plucked out a book, handing it to me. The title was *The Star People*. "Take this home and read it. Star Children are put here to help humans in their evolution to be better beings, more caring and kind. More considerate of one another, other species, and the earth. Star Children are highly intuitive, can sense spirits and even know when something is going to happen before it does. They are our shamans, our guides."

I was intrigued but failed to see how she could consider me with any of these abilities. I had talked about my "knowing" some things before they happen, but I just figured I was tuned into physical or language cues more than others. Maybe from being an only child growing up in a world of dramatic adults. When I told her this she said, "Yes! That's how it happens, this knowing and the physical and language cues are part of it!"

According to the authors, aliens from somewhere in the universe placed Star Children here, but often these children have no idea what they really are. This nagging uncertainty makes them feel out of place, but they also have extraordinary abilities, such as great empathy; they can heal themselves and others; they are "awake," meaning aware that humans are not the sole sentient beings in the universe. Whether or not I was ready to believe as she did didn't matter to her; what did matter was that I didn't scoff. She enjoyed the fact that I would ask questions and seriously consider her answers.

One day she called me to tell me that she had been diagnosed with breast cancer. The devastation rippled through me, rendering me speechless. I stammered, but the thought running through my mind was how unfair this diagnosis was, given what she had gone through. A few years before her diagnosis, Maria, who admitted she felt oddly compelled to bend to society's idea of beautiful, especially if you need a husband, had surgery for breast implants. The implants were made by Dow Corning, filled with a gelatin solution (this was before saline). The implant had obscured a spot of cancer, until it grew to a later stage.

I was so upset I don't remember what I said to her. Finally, a week later, I called her, feeling guilty at my lack of support for her when she told me the diagnosis. I said, "I cannot find the strength to say what I need to say. I'm overwhelmed." She laughed and generously said, "No shit, Sherlock." I felt even more horrible that here I was tongue-tied, again, and she had the grace and humor to make a smart ass comment back. I marveled at her ability to defuse a difficult situation.

A few months later, my husband was transferred back home, and Maria and her husband remained in Texas to be near her oncologist until she was declared clear of cancer. Once her doctor released her, she and her husband moved to Maryland, and to my delight I lived only six hours away. I made the drive to her home a couple times over the next two years. Her youngest son was out of the house by then.

Our conversations about everything paranormal and normal resumed. For me, it was lovely to have someone think of me as talented—she deeply admired my writing skills and often asked that I write her story and publish it, trusting that I would do her life story justice. I was a good way from feeling the same confidence she had about my writing, but I was flattered she'd think so highly of me and my ability. Healing, and what she thought was my gift to do so, came up from time to time, but I failed to take it seriously. I had no idea how I was supposed to heal anyone. I understood the process; I didn't, however, understand the capacity for one person, at a distance even, to affect the physical body of another. Despite the fact that Edgar Cayce apparently had that skill, I simply didn't know what I was supposed to *really* do. And in the back of my mind I kept thinking of the burden the healing could become if it didn't work. I suppose if I truly believed then it would always work, would it not? She understood my trepidation, she always told me. The best healers, she said, *should* doubt, but that didn't mean I didn't have the developed ability. She felt everyone did to some extent, but a Star Child would be cautious, as the ego simply is more humble. I was flattered, but still not sure.

Then her husband was transferred to Cairo, Egypt, as an inspector at a power plant. She had been there a year when she emailed me and asked me to come visit her. I was thrilled. At that point, I had been in Canada and Mexico, but nowhere overseas.

Maria was back in the states alone visiting her children, so when it was time to leave for Egypt, she met me at Dulles Airport. From there we continued on Air France to Paris, where we had a day and a half layover, and then on to Cairo. In the hotel, we discovered they did not provide washcloths. We went downstairs to the lobby desk. She asked in English if we could have washcloths. The woman behind the counter, who suddenly didn't speak anything but French (she had spoken English when we arrived), said, "Non." That made Maria angry. "Could you at least tell us where we could buy washcloths nearby?" The woman merely shrugged.

"Well! We'll see about that." I trotted behind her as she stormed to the elevator to go back to our room. Once there, Maria grabbed the bath mat, found her scissors (this was before 9/11) and cut up the mat into four nice wash clothes, handing me two. We popped open a fine bottle of French wine we'd bought in the lobby and proceeded to laugh our asses off all evening. We'd show the French! This event wasn't the only time I saw a bit of edge to Maria, but it was always in the face of what she considered injustice.

The next day we decided to explore Paris. We boarded a bus, which flew around corners on two wheels, it seemed, and stopped at crosswalks nearly standing the thing up on its nose, sending anyone standing flying down the aisle. They'd get up, dust themselves off, and without a word, grab the overhead straps and we'd continue on. Maria and I were amazed that, unlike Americans, the French didn't seem outraged. Maria laughed, "And here I was angry over the lack of washcloths!"

Arriving at the train station, we boarded the train into Paris. We'd purchased our tickets at the hotel, so we were set … we thought. After a few miles, I heard the conductor intone, "Terminus, terminus!" I told Maria: "That means the end. We are coming to the end of this line. We're not going into Paris." Maria said, "Oh, don't be silly! See the map on the wall? It shows this line going all the way into the heart of Paris." Sadly my translation was correct. The conductor came through and punched our tickets as the train came to a stop. Sure enough, we had to disembark in the village Aulnay Sous-Bois, which meant, in my extremely rusty college French, "something under brush." I later researched and found the idiom meant "under the woods." Nevertheless, we set out gamely for an exploration. Another train would not come through for a couple hours.

We were hungry and stopped in a little hole-in-the-wall sandwich shop where the young proprietor was eager to speak to us in English and

I tried to speak to him in French. I amused him with my efforts. Maria and I had *steak hashé, avec fries*. Americans would recognize it as a Philly Cheese Steak, but with the fries on top the sandwich. It was delicious.

We walked around the neighborhood, noting its eighteenth century structures, the beautiful homes, tree-lined streets. Coming around one corner, I spotted a cherry red, 1957 Chevy; it sparkled in the sun and was in pristine restored shape. Maria stood back amused as I approached, noting the shiny chrome, the red leather seats, the spectacular fins. Then I heard a soft whistle. I looked up and around. The whistle came again, and I realized it was coming from the house behind me. A young man was on the second floor, leaning over his balcony. He waved to let me know he was the one who whistled, and the owner of that not-to-be-touched '57 Chevy.

I waved, gestured toward the car saying: "*Magnifique!*" and Maria laughed, linked arms with me, and we scurried away, comrades in mischief.

All too soon we boarded the train. Once in Paris, my efforts at French amused more than a few Parisians. We walked in awe under the Eiffel Tower, enjoyed the gardens, ate hotdogs in tube buns, and jumped the turnstile, Maria's idea, to get back on the train because we didn't understand the schedules. The next day we flew to Cairo.

In Maria's apartment, she settled me in my bedroom and then went to hers to unpack. She told me her husband would be home in a few hours for dinner. When I'd finished unpacking, I came out into the living room and on to the balcony to watch the street below. I heard her behind me and came back inside, ready to question, and exclaim about all I'd seen so far. But she had come to a standstill, near the dining room table, a negligee dangling from her hand. She said, "I found this hanging on a nail behind the bedroom door. It's not mine."

I had no idea what to say. I watched her, expectant, dread building. "I've suspected he was seeing someone. She called here once …"

"Are you sure?" I squeaked, a pitiful response in light of the seriousness of the discovery.

"I asked him about her. All he would say was she was a friend of a friend." My mind was a jumble of thoughts—what must be her dismay, her hurt and then I thought—what could this mean? Would she leave? I immediately realized that not only did I not know the language, I didn't even know how to call the airport, book a flight, or how to get there. My mind came back to the present, to see her gaze still locked on the gown.

As if my nervous energy broke through to her, she looked at me, suddenly dropped her hand with the gown, letting it hang by her side. "Well, this will have to be sorted out at another time. For now, you're here, I'm going to show you Cairo and we're going to have fun." On that last part, her voice rose, and I think she was determined to convince herself as well as me.

I didn't know what to say. She smiled, breaking the tension. "Let's fix dinner!" I felt so sorry for her, but also bewildered. Never had I encountered anything like this.

When her husband came home, there was not a flicker of anger, or dismay, or grief, absolutely no reaction to what she'd discovered. Perhaps that would come later, after I flew home. The dinner went well, with us regaling him with our travails and adventures in Paris. He especially delighted in the washcloth story. I relaxed, taking my cue from her.

For the next week, Maria showed me Cairo. We ventured out to visit amazing antiquities and museums. I learned how to haggle, as a respectful way to shop in the ancient marketplace, the Khan El Khalili.

She and her husband took me to sail on a *faluka*, Arabic for sail boat, and I heard crocodiles grunting at the edges of the Nile. She teased me mercilessly when the 50 something faluka's pilot, Captain Abdul, flirted with me, apparently inquiring in Arabic if I would like a whole pack of cigarettes. Maria's husband laughed and said: "Wow! He must really like you. A whole pack!" They had a good laugh at my expense, and the "no" shake of my head let the Captain know I wasn't interested.

We visited her little "rug man" who lived in a tiny hut beside the road in her neighborhood. I bought two camel hair rugs and he gave me *baksheesh*, or tip, of a fresh sprig of rosemary he had grown in a tiny garden. I couldn't help but notice his tubular shaped teeth, perfectly rounded off on the tops. Maria told me it was because the grinding sand was ever-present, and it even got into the food.

She was amused at my awe of the pyramids of Giza and the Sphinx when I blurted out I thought it would be bigger, or when I put my hand on one massive stone of the largest Pyramid, that of the Pharaoh Khufu. I wondered whether he had put his hand on the same spot. I realized that to Maria, far more traveled, I was her acolyte, to whom she was showing the world.

My understanding of Maria deepened on this trip. While she had her own secrets, she had learned to not only weather betrayal, but also to grow beyond the grief, the hurt. Her calm demeanor was practiced, and she believed that each of us has a unique journey and that we can learn from others' journeys. Although I never said anything to her, I felt she was at times standing back, watching me travel on my own quest as she cheered from the starting gate.

When she and her husband returned from Egypt, they moved to Maryland again. Not long after, Maria became embroiled in the Dow Corning class action lawsuits regarding the breast implants. She told me about her meeting with the lawyers and just how grueling the questioning would be on the stand. Her testimony may or may not net a monetary gain, and she said, "Of course, even if we women win our cases, most of the money will go to the lawyers." That is eventually what happened. The case prevailed against Dow Corning, but her check was around $50,000. I knew it was little compensation for her stress and discomfort.

My husband and I spent the weekend with them once, but mostly we continued our connection through email. Our subject matters were our lives at the time and about the paranormal, or the Star Children, or the idea of healing, though not as much as in the past. And then she was diagnosed with cancer again.

This time, it was in the bone, in her hip. She couldn't sit or even lie down comfortably. Her emails turned to asking me to consider my "gift" and heal her from a distance; all I had to do was imagine white light surrounding her and to say out loud: "Please heal Maria from her cancer. Stop her pain." I did not know whom I was imploring (she always said the energy of the universe) or even if I was doing it right.

After a few months, she was declared cancer free. I couldn't say her healing had anything to do with me. I must have been a miserable excuse for a Star Child to her. I chose to do more research and came to realize there might be something to healing. Yet, I couldn't shake the feeling of failure. If I really could heal, and maybe had I been more pro-active, the cancer would not have returned. I supposed one has to truly believe. Because of her, I began to think about belief and what it cost, what it brought to you, what it took away. How hard it was to maintain. Over and over I thought: I must be careful that whatever it is I believe it does not turn into rigid dogma, not allowing me to think beyond a linear path. I think she finally sensed my reluctance, as she only mentioned healing to me one more time, later.

They moved again, this time to the state where her adoptive parents were living and aging, needing someone to look after them. I asked about her sister and the possibility that she might help care for their parents. She told me only that her sister remained angry and resentful about the past.

I don't know that I would have had the strength she did to live in her parents' home and take care of them, given what had happened long ago. I asked her how she felt about caring for a man who had brutally abused her. She said: "He's old now. He can't do anything anymore." I detected a sense of satisfaction in her voice, she even chuckled. Ultimately, it came down to the practical of what needed to be done. Her father passed away first then later her mother. She talked about the dispersing of their household, but nothing of what the stay might have cost her.

In 2001, she and her husband moved so he could work at a chemical plant. She was a mere 30 minutes away, living in a rented house. I did visit with her three times in the eight months they were there. She told me on the first visit that she'd located her birth mother living nearby and that she'd been to see her.

"How did that go?" I asked.

"Well, it was okay. But I have to limit contact with her. My real father passed away some years ago, and she's in really bad health— diabetes, heart condition, overweight. I wasn't there long when she asked me for money. I gave her some, what I had on me, but I knew I won't be going back. Her need is great ... Well, I can see where the asking probably won't end."

I felt so sad for Maria, although she seemed to take it in stride, as if she was immune to all the bad stuff. "What did she say, or did you ask her, about giving you up for adoption and your grandfather selling you and your sister?"

Maria laughed, her warm brown eyes cast down. "I didn't really ask her. From what I understand she's never had much of anything, very little education, probably under the control of her father ... She wasn't forthcoming; I guess it was so long ago she's put it out of her mind." I will remember always the rise of her head as she finished telling me this, the turning her face toward the sun that beamed into her kitchen. The resolution that became set on her features.

But then her mood brightened, as I'd seen it do many times when we were talking about dark things. It occurred to me that the humor appeared whenever the conversation turned toward a devastating realization. I think she showed me one type of fuel for bravery: the engine of it is fed with humor and, in turn the anger burns out.

In 2002, my emails trailed off to Maria and each of us wrote sporadically. I felt at fault as I was slower to respond than she. Then she wrote to say the cancer had returned again in her bones. She told about one day when she writhed on the bed in agony, when the dresser drawers came flying out and onto the floor, as if they were shoved violently from inside the chest. Unseen energy, she said, can manifest physically and our will has the power to move things.

Moving physical objects is one thing, but banishing illness is another, I thought. She did not ask me to heal her. A bit stubborn, and worried, I nevertheless told her I imagined her embraced in a brilliant white and gold light. She said to me: "Kiddo, I don't think even your ability to heal will work this time."

How on earth could I have fallen to sporadic communication, yet as we moved into 2003, my own life's travails distracted me—the deaths of my parents, my daughter's leaving for college, our house move, beginning a new degree, just change after change. I lost track of Maria, my friend, my confidant.

On Thanksgiving 2004, I took a break from cooking the family turkey and trimmings and went to my computer. For some reason, Maria was on my mind. It had been several months since I'd been in contact with her. I felt a vague sense of unease. I emailed her and it bounced back. I found her phone number but it was disconnected. With a deep dread, I returned to the computer and googled her name. Her obituary came up immediately.

She died in July 2003. Her short obituary said she was buried in her husband's home state. Guilt overwhelmed me. How can someone so powerful, so bigger than life just pass away and I not know it for over a year? Where was my so-called intuition? Why did none of our mutual friends mention it? How could I be so neglectful?

My thoughts rambled through scenes of sitting and talking intimately with her about our fears. How parents betray, and sometimes husbands. How some friends don't always understand. She had a firm path on which to travel that she had learned to navigate over the years, but it was not a path she ever forced me upon. She simply showed me her way, which is after all, only one way.

As my sorrow sank in, I accepted a new thought: I had not needed Maria as a teacher, a guide any more. I sensed that with her illness worsening she was also letting go, that she knew it was time to go. I think her final lesson for me, one that she either talked about explicitly or that informed all her conversations, was that nothing on earth is permanent, save energy. It does not die, this energy that we are, but will manifest in myriad ways. I'll see her in the cardinal that comes to my feeder, the cloud that is shaped like a rabbit, the puff of smoke that rises from a chimney that comes from burning a log that came from a living tree.

I am a better person because of my friend. She reinforced in me that seeking is our right and our duty. She taught me what belief is, even if that belief, or what I could grasp of it, was not perfect. She taught me to trust my own intuition. And I feel lucky to have watched her manifest her own self-empowerment.

Maria the Star Child is returned to the universe, her job here finished.

I am doing great. Thanks for asking
— *Madison Samis*

My Own Eyes

DIANA HUME GEORGE

||||||||||||||||||||||||||||||||||||||||||||||||||||||||||||||||||||||||||||||||

For Malcolm A. Nelson, died December 25, 2018

It's hard to talk to a ghost. At first a part of your mind feels watched by another corner of yourself you let someone else own. After a while you feel less judged as a survivor.
—*Roger Clay Palmer to a grieving friend*

To think of a life story as a compendium of memories that one is free to interpret according to the demands (and desires) of the present seems to me characteristic of a writer's way of thinking. ...The strange thing is how many of us want to fix the account, by repeating over and over, to ourselves and to others, one or another preferred version.
—*J.M. Coetzee, The Good Story*

In the final parting what became rust turns to gold, and all our errors are revealed. ...Every important death for those left behind is a kind of phoenix. ...We are born to a new self; the birth is painful, long, and tentative. Write while the pain is hot. Later, as it fades, you cannot quite recall what it felt like.
—*Luciana Bohne to me after Mac's death*

Mac Nelson 1980s, photo by Diana Hume George

Part I: I don't trust memory.

But I've invested half my life in its mercies as the best form of immortality we can approximate. Since I do not believe in any gods or an afterlife of individual consciousness, I've always thought of memory on the page as the way to keep people we love alive beyond their bodily habitation. People die and we bring them back to life, resurrect them through the way they gestured, the curve of lip as they said that, what you heard as your head lay in her lap on the evening porch, how that day she turned to you at the kitchen table and said six words you have always remembered, how he angled his hand when he walked away.

Other comforts come to us in less individual form because matter cannot be created or destroyed. The iron in our blood comes from the death of supernovas. Bodies decay into the soil that feeds trees. I have thought that it's possible to get past the need to rescue individuals. I've long since realized it's *all* temporary, that there will come a day in the future of the cosmos that even Shakespeare's work will no longer exist. If Buddhism has done me any good, it's in understanding that someday, we'll all be as if we never existed. That's how it also was *before* we emerged from eternity into time; we all return to nothingness. What a wonderful thing that we are here at all, for this lovely moment. Maybe William Blake was right, that there's immutable Imagination beyond time and space. Yet I've come to be sustained by benevolent nothingness. When I look at the stars at night and feel small, that's not scary any more.

But no, that's not enough comfort, is it, it's not endurance of the mortal, corporeal self that we try lifelong to understand, our own or, just as vitally, the mysterious identity of those we love. For we who write personally, finding words to bring back our people on the page can be a passion. While we live, we are in that world where beloved fellow mortals come and go, and where, in our lifetimes, we lose those we love before we lose ourselves. Sometimes we part from them during our lives. Oh that rending—people who were once deeply bonded, lovers or spouses, siblings or parents, parting in bitterness, lost to each other forever in this mortal moment.

This happened to me with a person I once loved as I love life itself. Mac Nelson was my soulmate, though we have long since separated. He died just weeks ago, quiet and quick on Christmas Day. In his mid-eighties he was surely old enough to have had a fulsome life, but no one can imagine him gone, as hundreds of his former students and present friends have written online, calling him a force of nature, a giant, the most memorable man they ever knew, one who filled every room he entered, influenced every life he touched. He had an earlier legal wife with whom he'd had children, and a wife in between me and his current wife Joyce—the man lived a long time. I call Joyce his wife, though they never made it legal. Nor did he and I, but wife I was, for twenty long years, as Joyce is now. I have the greatest respect for their bond.

But it is time I paid overdue respect to the bond between me and Mac as well. And because of how we later parted, for decades I have not. Mac first entered my life as my Shakespeare and poetry professor when I was nineteen, and in my early twenties he became my lover and housemate and partner. We raised kids and dogs and cats. We had a garden of greens from which I made salads. We heated mostly with wood we chopped. We built a communal household of people who passed through our lives, or stayed in contact for years, like our artist friends Dori and Terry, our Buddhist buddy Pat, and always Richard, whom I met in my first class of Mac's. Or folks who lived with us summers, like my best friend Nancy, her husband Mark, their daughter Kris, who became Mac's and my daughter of sorts. We launched annual camping trips in leaky old tents for a month at a time, to Cape Cod and out west, Colorado and New Mexico, the Grand Canyon and Arches, Canyonlands and Yosemite, Mesa Verde and Yellowstone.

The book for which I'm best known, *The Lonely Other, A Woman Watching America,* was partly about our travels together. After tromping through churches in England and cemeteries in Massachusetts, we co-authored a field guide, *Epitaph and Icon,* about 18th century American gravestones. We once were a golden couple in our little corner of academe, where we shone just brightly enough to be remembered by dozens of our former students and colleagues and the people we met on our travels, and to be mourned, when we parted, by friends who felt somehow betrayed because our partnership had inspired their own sense of the possible.

It was I who left, and the leaving was bitter. I walked out my own front door and blew up our mutual life behind me. We'd both thought that we'd be together until death did us part, that his would be the last face I saw as I died, or more likely, given the difference in our ages, mine would be his—among the ironies of our lives, he and poet Donald Hall used to exchange letters about Don's fear of that when he was first married to Jane Kenyon. So our end was a death of its own. In the end, the residual effects of our initial connection, me as his student when he taught me all I know about literature, got the better of us. I couldn't remain his acolyte, and he could not quite allow me to grow up. So I left our home in Brocton, New York, the universe we'd built, where he remained until his death some thirty years later. In the early years of our estrangement, he barely spoke to me, feeling that I had betrayed and nearly destroyed him—and I felt that he had done the same to me. I used to blame him for not being able to grow and change. But it is time I hold myself equally responsible.

That is why I don't trust memory, the only tool we have to dig up our old bones. Memory mutates, it exacerbates insults, it transforms realities, forgets facts, revises history. As Daniel Schacter puts it, memory "sins." It misattributes, it projects and displaces. I have watched that process in my friends, students, fellow writers, observed how people forget their own sins against love in the effort to declare their innocence. I have seen it in myself. Even though some of what I subsequently published about us was fair, several pieces I wrote in the wake of our parting cast me as martyr, him as manipulator. Neither is really true.

Most writers who are veterans of past partnerships that end badly construct a narrative with ourselves as the victims, heroes, or martyrs. When I left him and our world, I wasn't mature enough to realize that's what writers, what *people,* almost always do; we back-construct stories in which we occupy the roles that suit us best as our own main characters. It can be lethal, this tendency. It surely was with us. The end and the aftermath were so bitter, so full of pain for us both that we stayed away from each other, trapped in our own mutually exclusive narratives about how much we'd each loved the other, how the other had betrayed our trust. What an expense of spirit. What a waste of shame.

For almost a decade, silence reigned between us except for his continued participation in the life of my son, who had become his son. He has remained a fine father; a few years ago, he and Bernie went on a backcountry canoe and camping trip in Yellowstone. But not once did he and I have a conversation, undefended and mutually compassionate, about what had occurred between us. Not once. He married. He divorced. I did not marry or divorce, but I had two partners before the wondrous one I've now been with for even longer than I was with Mac. Not least of John's virtues: he understands Mac's place in my history, even in my present. Regularly over the years, he's listened patiently as I awake from yet another dream in which I'm back in my old world with Mac, and these dreams are never good.

In recent years, Mac and I at last rebuilt a tentative friendship, in which I often edited his writing for him and we continued mutual contact with people we'd at first divvied into *his* and *hers.* Once he even signed an email "Love, Mac," and I choked back tears. We saw each other once a year, at his house or my cottage, with the extended family we'd built over the years, including grandchildren. Ours became one of those common stories of coming partway toward each other in later life. People sometimes do this, but just as often, oftener, hostilities never cease, issues frozen in the past becoming the plots of novels and of movies, and more sadly, of real lives—long entombed events are dug up anew at family dinner tables because old agendas, sometimes a single sentence once uttered in anger, remain imprinted in people's secret hearts.

Just because we reconnected didn't mean we ever worked things out. His terms were clear: we would not ever speak of the past. This condition for our renewed contact—in recent years, we emailed at least twice a week—was costly, not that he didn't have a right to exact it (he did), but I never stopped wanting us to understand our past. He never stopped wanting to avoid opening that old wound. So I remained frozen in that stuck place in my heart where we'd parted, those wounds more heartfelt than the togetherness had been. Writer Richard Lehnert, who credits Mac as a deep influence on his early life, wrote me in the wake of this death, suspecting I'd trap myself in this old agenda.

Your complex grief for Mac will no doubt come and go at various intensities and intervals, for the foreseeable future if not the rest of your

life. You know this. What I'm about to offer is, god help me, advice, and
of the worst kind—unsolicited. Whatever clumsiness I commit, I do only
because I love you. If you find yourself trying to Figure It All Out For
Once And For All, it might be a good idea to remind yourself that that's
not going to happen. ...You were two flawed human beings attempting to
do the best you could in difficult situations with limited tools. It's time to
rest in that.

Here and now, I vow to rest— I'm not ever going to figure out
what happened, how either of us could have abandoned the labor
of love we had built together. Instead I want to allow memory its
resurrective grace. When we became bitter and angry, we lost our
knowledge of when we were "my own eyes" to each other, as the first
Queen Elizabeth called the Earl of Leicester, which Mac, a Renaissance
scholar, applied to us. Excavating memory to help write his obituary,
I recalled events from eons ago. Old friends recollected the years
we were in love. I've not had access to these memories in decades,
and now, speaking to people who remember our salad days better
than I do, going through old photographs from his albums, reading
excerpts from the ongoing journal he kept when we had to be apart for
professional trips, they suffuse me. They're painful. They're lovely.

Part II: The Memories

Mac and Diana, 1970s, photo by Nancy Luce

I want to be known, and I think you want to know me. I want to let you know how strong my urge for you, for life. I want to hold and be held, behold and be beheld.

On an old blanket on a rocky beach on Lake Erie eating cottage cheese with Lawry's seasoned salt and Frank's hot sauce, Mac's face turned toward late afternoon sun.

This scholarly man with Bach in his blood, cross-legged in front of the stereo inhaling Cat Stevens, Led Zeppelin, Moody Blues.

Before every trip, as we pulled out of the driveway, van loaded with tents and gear, his voice booming out the window, "Wagons Ho!"

I am a convincing son of a bitch, am I not? I've got myself conned into believing I know some things. I love to woo you. Woo-woo.

In Bob Marley's "three little birds," his musicology meets his politics.

Mac's first words as a toddler after three years of silence: "Grandfather, look at the moon."

Telescope set up on the deck and the side yard for Boy Scouts and neighbor kids, showing them the constellations—that's Cassiopeia—ending with the double star Albireo, everyone in awe.

My warm forcefield, my soft rock, after these many years I am still giddy with wooing you, you make me new over and again, you renew me and I make you fresh, ever strange, ever home and familiar.

Singing Bonnie Raitt all over America. "Your sweet and shiny eyes are like the stars above Laredo, like meat and potatoes to me. In my sweet dreams we are in a bar and it's my birthday, drinking salty margaritas with Fernando."

The summer of "All Night Long," me and Mac and my friend Nancy dancing on the deck, me watching them watching me, each watching each other, all night long, in some sort of love.

Feet up on our outside table at a cook-out, the kids giggling at "Pass the mucking fargarine."

If I had to choose between letting the big wild bear inside me out to play, and just talking to you, just touching and kissing and looking, you know what I'd pick. But I don't want to choose. Sure, bears are dangerous, but they're good.

Arriving on Cape Cod each May, stopping at every old Massachusetts burying ground to rub the slates, our favorite a crude fieldstone to an infant daughter, "MARY DR to IRA ATKINS HAR 14 DAYS 1744," to whom we dedicate our field guide on old gravestones.

On the Cape and The Vineyard, Ted Harper, Tom and Marilyn Bridwell, Linda Kelsey and Glenn Strand, Judy Cressy and Dingy Watson, meeting in the basement of the Brewster General Store reading poems, part of the Cape's off-season life, carpenters and set builders, writers and actors, below the radar.

Rafting Quivet Creek on the Cape with Tom in a blow-up boat, digging clams for dinner.

My father plays solitaire, drinks Manhattans in his pajamas. I'm not ready for pajamas and solitaire. I don't own any stinking pajamas.

Out our dining room window, armored jousting on horseback in the side yard, Society for Creative Anachronism knights drafting our Bernie and Krissy as their pages.

Teaching any group of bodies standing near him to sing rounds. "White sand and gray sand" and "Old Abra'm Brown is dead and gone, you'll never see him more! He used to wear a long brown coat that buttoned down before."

Walking the mesa top together near Grand Junction, eager to buy those 40 acres of Uncompahgre Plateau looking out over canyonlands into Utah, certain we would someday come to stay.

Love, you are everywhere I look. I speak not here of your profound thoughts, nor of your estimable salsa, nor even your astonishing lips, though I wish to feast on all of these.

Teaching the kids to hang the food high from a tree in camp so as not to attract bears, watching their eyes fill with magical fear.

Walking through Delicate Arch in moonlight, Slough Creek at Yellowstone, the kids eating Fruit Loops at Yosemite.

In the sun on our deck in January as in June, face always raised to that warmth he worshipped, eyes closed, shortwave tuned to Tottenham Hotspur in London, the Cubs in Chicago.

With you I am an active verb, a progressive tense. You turn me deponent, passive, past tense, depleted gerund. I grow active again. I am become verb, creator of worlds. It's unseemly for a mature man to carry on the way I do about you.

To Bernie's girlfriend Mary Ellen walking up the stairs in her bikini, age 15, tan and gorgeous: "Get some birth control!"

Arriving at the Cape, Mac driving the brown Dodge van, me sleeping in the big back bed, calling himself driver of "Cleopatra in her barge."

Presiding in the ballroom of the mansion where we were caretakers, then the farmhouse, listening to Firesign Theater, watching Monty Python, running our little commune: Richard the poet, David the FBI agent, Katie the writer, Peter the veteran, Larry who loved Patty, Deb the thruway toll taker, John the oboe player, Susan the student, Jeannie the nurse, Ruth who sold Mary Kay, Kim the knight, all long gone their separate ways.

I'm not much good without you. It's time, just time with you I want, to dream in your face, look into your long eyes, my own. The older I get, the more I know what matters in this rackety life—I want to talk with you, eat with you, listen to music, sit in the sun, make love.

Krissy leaning out the window at Yellowstone, ecstatic at a herd of buffalo, Bernie on his belly among the prairie dogs. Without him, the kids would never see such creatures.

Bernie and Mary Ellen climbing among ancient redwoods at Sequoia, years before they name their daughter after the trees.

First dozens, then more than a hundred albums of clippings and photos recording our travels, the father's artform in our home.

I wish this plane would land so I can get back to you, back to the garden of us, barefoot. You are where I place my love and dreams, my stars and dirt. Writing to you is foreplay, five or six or ten play, everything's play, I am indeed a child again.

In England, a night on the floor of Gatwick airport during a strike, first trapped on an escalator where Mac loses his balance. Bernie behind him hears him as he falls backwards, "Excuse me, pardon me, Madam."

Ever hear the one about the vicar, he asked? I had not. TO THE WOODS! said the man. NO NO! cried the maid. TO THE WOODS! said the man. NO NO! cried the maid, I'LL TELL THE VICAR! The man: MY CHILD, I AM THE VICAR.

"You're the deepest person I know," I said. He replied, "A case of mistaken identity, my dear, I'm smart but I'm shallow."

You cast me as Prospero, magician, and I become magic. But he knows better: We are such stuff as dreams are made on, and our little life is rounded with a sleep. He knows, but I don't. You won't lose me, until my little life is rounded with a sleep. Be with me now, while I am still in the sun, while I am someone.

Toward the end of us, our dog Alfie brings us back together over his dying. We sit with him as he labors, first to live and then to die. We weep when he is gone and dig a hole to bury him, throwing roses over his body. Standing there, Mac sings to me from the opera *Candide*. "We'll build our house and chop our wood, and make our garden grow...."

But we could not. I wish we had been kinder to each other in life, but I have this chance to be kind to us now. I'd thought an entire era of my life was lost to me, and I am grateful beyond words that these words have restored it to me. I have empathy and compassion for the two much younger people who sojourned together many years, and better, I feel renewed love for our faulty mortal selves, we who found each other in each other's eyes. I don't feel discontinuity between me and that young woman—I am she, grown older now. So let these words be our house, our garden. And may this elegy to an old love recall for you your own old loves— father or mother, lover or friend, sister or brother—with whom you once shared a house, a garden.

Mac Nelson, 1980s, photo by Diana Hume George

Diana Hume George takes the common threads of human existence—love, loss, aging, grief, and identity—and gives them uncommon clarity and depth. Her writing reminds us of the limits of light and dark, and of the complexities of everyday emotions that shape and sometimes haunt us for a lifetime. In this beautiful tribute to a former partner, she inspires us to live and love big, and to honor every moment of our lives.

— VICTORIA STOPP, Author of *Hurting Like Hell, Living with Gusto: My Battle with Chronic Pain*

Biographies

COLLEEN ANDERSON owns Mother Wit Writing and Design, a creative studio in Charleston. She writes poems, essays, fiction, nonfiction, and songs. Her recent publications are *Missing: Mrs. Cornblossom*, an award-winning children's chapter book, and *Bound Stone*, a poetry chapbook.

LAURA TREACY BENTLEY is a poet and a novelist. She is the author of *The Silver Tattoo, Night Terrors: A Short Story Prequel, Looking for Ireland: An Irish-American Pilgrimage*, and *Lake Effect*. Laura has been widely published in the United States and Ireland. lauratreacybentley.com

DALEEN BERRY A *New York Times* best-selling author with seven books, Daleen is also an award-winning investigative journalist and newspaper columnist. She has given a TED talk and appeared on ABC, NBC, CBS, among other networks. Daleen enjoys blogging, and she's also written for the Associated Press, the BBC, the *Daily Beast*, and *Huffington Post*.

GRACE CAVALIERI is the Maryland Poet Laureate. She founded and still produces "The Poet and the Poem" for public radio celebrating 42 years on-air, now recorded at the Library of Congress. She's the monthly poetry columnist/reviewer (*"EXEMPLARS"*) for *The Washington Independent Review Of Books*. She lives and writes in Annapolis, Maryland. She has four grown daughters, four grandchildren, and a great-grandchild.

SHEILA COLEMAN-CASTELLS is a former professor, researcher, current consultant to governments and industry, and advocate for the underserved in the fields of Education, Workforce Development and Labor. She writes as a new Affrilachian who is the mother of a beloved twenty-something son, and she chose West Virginia as her new family home over a decade ago, and hasn't looked back. She lives on a holy mountaintop in Preston County.

LYDIA A. CYRUS is a writer from Huntington, West Virginia. She'd rather be barefoot and with the trees of her homeland, but for now she lives in Lafayette, Indiana. She likes the Midwest just fine but she misses the coyotes and lions greatly.

KATE DOOLEY writes short stories, long fiction, and poetry. Her novel, *Hears the Wind* won first place in its category in WV Writers Competition in 1995. She shares her poetry at open mic and stays active with local writers in Lewisburg.

After years of negotiating a culture unresponsive to feminine creative energies, JEANETTE LUISE EBERHARDY PhD, MFA began to listen to her own imagination, and, slowly, her passion for writing emerged. Now working as a writer, storyteller, speaker, and educator at Massachusetts College of Art and Design, Eberhardy encourages others to bring forward their authentic voice. Eberhardy can be reached at wivinc.com.

JANICE GARY writes memoir and nonfiction in an attempt to understand the confounding crazy, beautiful world we all live in. Her memoir, *Short Leash* (MSU Press, 2013) braids together trauma recovery, the natural world, a protective dog and rock 'n roll through a walk in the park that becomes a path of healing. She teaches in the Master of Liberal Studies Program at Arizona State University and conducts workshops at various sites around the country including The Writers Center Bethesda, MD, The Studios of Key West and for the International Women's Writing Guild.

DIANA HUME GEORGE is the author or editor of ten books of nonfiction, poetry, and literary criticism, including *The Lonely Other* and *Oedipus Anne: The Poetry of Anne Sexton*. She is Professor of English Emerita at Penn State University, Behrend College, where she founded the Women's and Gender Studies program, as well as the Creative Writing program. Former co-director of Chautauqua Writers' Festival, she's a contributing editor of *Chautauqua Journal*. Since 1999, she's been affiliated with Goucher College's MFA program in Nonfiction.

ANGELA GIRON is the Assistant Director and a Clinical Assistant Professor of the Masters of Liberal Studies Program at Arizona State University. Ms. Giron has worked professionally in Theatre and Film out of Chicago, Los Angeles, New York, Montreal and Toronto, Canada. Among her many TV and film credits, one of her favorite portrayals was in the role of Alice B. Toklas in the film, *The Moderns* (1988) directed by Alan Rudolph. She performed her most recently authored play, *Nitza—A Cuban Flavor* at the United Solo Festival, NYC, in October 2016. She lives in South Phoenix, Arizona.

MAGIN LASOV GREGG's essays have appeared in *The Washington Post, The Dallas Morning News, Bellingham Review, The Rumpus, River Teeth's Beautiful Things, Under the Gum Tree, Full Grown People*, and elsewhere. *Solstice* Literary Magazine named her essay "The Gleaming Miraculous" as an Editor's Pick and finalist in its 2018 summer contest judged by Phillip Lopate. Her first essay about Lyme Disease ("To Punctuate" *Full Grown People*) was nominated for a Pushcart Prize in 2018.

Three times a Pushcart nominee, KARI GUNTER-SEYMOUR's chapbook *Serving* was chosen runner up in the *2016 Yellow Chair Review Annual Chapbook Contest* and nominated for a 2018 Ohioana Award. She is the founder/curator of the "Women of Appalachia Project," (womenofappalachia.com) an arts organization she created to address discrimination directed at women living in Appalachia. She is Poet Laureate for Athens, OH. karigunterseymourpoet.com.

DEBBIE HAGAN is book reviews editor for *Brevity* and author of *Against the Tide* (Hamilton Books, 2004). Her writing has appeared in *Harvard Review, Hyperallergic, Pleiades, Superstition Review, Brain, Child*, and elsewhere. She's a visiting lecturer at the Massachusetts College of Art and Design.

RAJIA HASSIB was born and raised in Egypt and moved to the United States when she was twenty-three. Her first novel, *In the Language of Miracles*, was a *New York Times* Editor's Choice and received an honorable mention from the Arab American Book Award. Her second novel, *A Pure Heart*, is forthcoming from Viking (Penguin) in August of 2019. She holds an MA in Creative Writing from Marshall University, and she has written for *The New York Times Book Review* and *The New Yorker* online. She lives in Charleston with her husband and two children.

CANDACE JORDAN is a West Virginian by transplant and by ancestry. The beauty of the state is a constant inspiration to her in her visual art and writing. Her partner, Bob, and her schnoodle, Buddy, are her boon companions.

REBECCA KIMMONS is a singer, photographer, painter, sometime actor, lifelong scrutinizer of West Virginians and their habits, and a reader of history. A resident of Charleston, West Virginia, where she operates a small artists/writers' retreat, she is Bill's wife, and mother of two grown children, Katelyn, and Christopher. This is her first published work of fiction.

ARIANA KINCAID is a graduate of the WVU College of Law, Alderson-Broaddus when it was still a lowly College, and Philip Barbour High School. She is currently an Assistant Prosecuting Attorney in

Kanawha County. She considers herself a dog person, which causes her husband consternation but pleases her daughter and dog, Hercules Mulligan, to no end.

KATHERINE MANLEY was born and raised in southern West Virginia and is an educator for Logan County Schools. Her writing has been featured in *Hamilton Stone Review, Traditions: A Journal of West Virginia Folk Culture and Educational Awareness,* and *The Guyandot Observer.* During her free time, she enjoys relaxing at the beach with her family or reading by a cozy fire.

The inspiration to write came to **ESTHER MASCHIO** in a dream telling her of a 'new color', no one on Earth had never seen or heard about before. Since 2003, Esther's annual Studio Residencies in Lucca, Italy, have inspired her to not only create visual arts but also to express herself in writing. For over twenty five years Maschio has taught printmaking, while mentoring groups and individuals via workshops, readings, and talks. Contact Esther at firstempressions@comcast.net.

MEG MATICH is a Reykjavik-based poet and translator. Her translations have appeared in or are forthcoming from *PEN America, Exchanges, Words Without Borders, Asymptote, Gulf Coast,* and others. In 2015, she received the PEN Heim Translation Fund grant for her translation of Magnús Sigurðsson's *Cold Moons* (Phoneme Media, 2017). She has received grants and fellowships from the Fulbright Commission, the DAAD, the Banff Centre, the Icelandic Literature Center, and Columbia University. She is currently the Madame/Director of Reykjavik's Rauða Skáldahúsið.

KAREN SALYER MCELMURRAY is the author of a memoir, *Surrendered Child,* and two novels, *Strange Birds in the Tree of Heaven* and *The Motel of the Stars.* With poet Adrian Blevins, she co-edited the essay collection, *Walk Till the Dogs Get Mean: Meditations on the Forbidden from Contemporary Appalachia*. McElmurray is from Hagerhill, Kentucky.

WENDY PETERS is a 5th grade teacher at Daniels Elementary School and a lifelong resident of West Virginia. She is a public education activist, bookworm and nature lover. She enjoys spending time with her husband Brandon and their son Matthew. 55 STRONG

CARTER TAYLOR SEATON is the author of two novels, *Father's Troubles*, and *amo, amas, amat...an unconventional love story*, numerous magazine articles, and several essays, short stories, and the non-fiction, *Hippie Homesteaders*. Her biography of the late Ken Hechler, *The Rebel in the Red Jeep*, was released by West Virginia University Press in 2017. Her latest book, *Me and MaryAnn* is a compilation of stories of her renegade childhood and youth.

JUDITH RAMSEY SOUTHARD is an early baby boomer who struggled through temporary classrooms and buildings being torn down or built for that generation from Pigeon Creek Elementary through West Virginia University and now worries about how strained public budgets will take care of that oncoming crowd of seniors. She retired after more than thirty years as an educator in Mingo County, West Virginia. Now she enjoys traveling, grannying, and writing while trying to become a more loving and compassionate human being.

M. LYNNE SQUIRES is an award-winning Urban Appalachian Author. Her books include *Looking Back at Charleston*, her memoir *Letters to My Son*, and *Mid-Century Recipes from Cocktails to Comfort Food*. Currently, she is learning to embrace her silver white hair, appreciate her coffee without sugar, and strives fervently, though in vain, to pet the feral cat she feeds daily.

MARY IMO-STIKE received her MFA from West Virginia Wesleyan College in 2015. Her poems have been published in many journals, she was nominated for a Pushcart Prize in 2017, and her chapbook *In and Out of the Horse Latitudes* was published in 2018 by Finishing Line Press. Mary is the co-creator of More Than Words, a monthly literary event in Hurricane, WV.

SHERRELL RUNNION WIGAL is a poet living along the Ohio River in Parkersburg, West Virginia. She has been widely published throughout the country. Much of Sherrell's poetry reflects her love, appreciation and connection to nature, as well as people and her cultural heritage.

KANDI WORKMAN is a lover of the Appalachian Mountains and its people. Kandi is a life-long resident of the southern West Virginia coalfields, where she is raising her three children. She is currently spending a year as a Highlander Appalachian Transition Fellow, serving with the nonprofit Step By Step, to learn about capitalism, just transition, and how to empower and help aid the healing of the hurting people of Appalachia by increasing youth's knowledge of entrepreneurship and creating awareness of trauma-informed care community development.

KAREN WORKMAN grew up in Fayette County, WV and completed a BS degree in Computer Science from WVU Institute of Technology, an MBA from Marshall University and the University of Pennsylvania's Wharton School of Business Executive Education program. Her professional career spans more than 25 years in the areas of organization development, human resources, leadership development and entrepreneurship. She enjoys supporting her community by serving on several boards and with her husband Steve, co-owns Blind Wizard and Hidden Creek Mercantile—two local WV businesses. Karen and Steve live in Hurricane, WV, with their two sons (Alec and Connor), a Lhasa Apso named Allie and a black cat called Hocus.

Editor's Biography

CAT PLESKA (nee Hodges) is a 7th generation Appalachian, an author, editor, publisher, educator and storyteller. Her memoir, *Riding on Comets*, was published in 2015 by West Virginia University Press. She has memoir and personal essays published in such literary magazines as *Still: the Journal*, *Heartwood Magazine*, *Hamilton Stone Review*, *Traditions*, as well as publishing articles in *Wonderful West Virginia* magazine, and is the author of nearly 40 essays for West Virginia Public Radio. In addition, she has reviewed books for *The Charleston Gazette* and West Virginia University Press. She teaches writing workshops throughout the region, provides keynote addresses, and speaks frequently about writing in all its forms. She is also a member of Women of Appalachia Project presenting her story, "Membrane Croup," throughout the Ohio Valley. She also has served as editor for the anthologies *Voices on Unity: Coming Together, Falling Apart* and *Fed from the Blade*. She lives in West Virginia with her husband, six cats, one elderly dog, and a beautiful daughter, Katie, who lives a few miles away.

> *Someone I loved once gave*
> *me a box full of darkness. It*
> *took me years to understand*
> *that this, too, was a gift.*
> — *Mary Oliver*

End Notes

[1] Women and Depression, *Harvard Health Letter*, May, 2011, Harvard Health Publishing

[2] https://www.ncbi.nlm.nih.gov/pmc/articles/PMC1586137/

[3] https://adaa.org/living-with-anxiety/women/facts

[4] Consumer Attorneys of California, "Urban Myths" https://www.caoc.org/index.cfm?pg=isstort

[5] *Los Angeles Times*, "Legal Urban Legends Hold Sway" http://articles.latimes.com/2005/aug/14/business/fi-tortmyths14

[6] Consumer Attorneys of California, "The McDonald's Hot Coffee Case" https://www.caoc.org/?pg=facts

[7] Wikipedia, "Liebeck v. McDonald's Restaurants" https://en.wikipedia.org/wiki/Liebeck_v._McDonald%27s_Restaurants

57005762R00126